Unconditional
GOOD NEWS

Unconditional
GOOD NEWS

Toward an Understanding of Biblical Universalism

by NEAL PUNT

GRAND RAPIDS
WILLIAM B. EERDMANS PUBLISHING COMPANY

Library of Congress Cataloging in Publication Data

Punt, Neal.
    Unconditional good news.

    1. Universalism — Biblical teaching.
2. Universalism.   I. Title.
BS680.U55P86   234   80-10458
ISBN 0-8028-1835-8

Contents

Foreword

THE universal and particular strands of God's saving love are woven into the tapestry of biblical revelation. Students of biblical revelation differ in their description of the patterns which they discern. Rev. Neal Punt has written a book in which he describes his perception of how the universal and particular strands of God's revelation concerning his saving love are intertwined.

Punt writes with restraint. He patiently probes the position of those with whom he disagrees, and gently nudges forward those whom he considers too narrow of vision to see the broad sweep of biblical universalism. In this book the reader finds no strident language or impatient argumentation. The author does not imply that the Reformed community needs to be verbally chastised for its narrow predestinarian vision. With his cautious approach he retains the unique wholeness of faith-experience. He holds in tension-filled unity that which the intellect often rejects as logical nonsense.

The goal of every student of the Bible should be to allow the Bible to say what it intends to say. In Scripture God tells us what he has done in Christ; what he is doing in the authentic event of preaching; and what he plans to complete when Christ comes again. When one tries to explicate with theological precision the gracious character, the God-glorifying content, the eschatological urgency of gospel preaching, together with the biblical warrant for that preaching, he undertakes a demanding task. This book adds a fresh, important, and attractive dimension to the continuing discussion. We owe it to ourselves to consider seriously this unique contribution of Rev. Punt.

Alexander C. DeJong
Oaklawn, Illinois

Preface

THE premise developed in this book is so basic to our understanding of the message of Scripture that it will undoubtedly provoke some serious questions in the mind of the reader. Most of these questions will be considered somewhere in this presentation. Therefore the reader is asked to read the entire book and then return to the sections that are of special interest to him. The first chapter sets forth our thesis. Chapters II through VII are concerned with biblical foundations. Chapters VIII through XIII develop some of the implications and practical applications of this new premise.

Although I have been thinking for many years about this premise and have spoken to various people about it, I have not used this approach either in my ministry or in my exposition of Scripture from the pulpit. This restraint is not because I consider this approach to be unscriptural or contrary to the creeds of my church. My only purpose in limiting my thoughts to private and now public discussion is that views which are chiefly a matter of one's own interpretation or understanding should not be promulgated as accepted Christian teaching. Until now, the views herein expressed have been much too limited in their exposure to the Christian community for me to have felt free to use them in my ministry.

If the reader finds the material presented in readable form this is due, in large measure, to Dr. Alexander C. DeJong, who graciously read each chapter as it was produced and offered his welcome criticism and constructive advice. The Rev. Winston C. Boelkins, neighbor and colleage, collaborated in this work so closely, literally paragraph by paragraph, that without his insights and counsel regarding format and expression as well as his constant encouragement, this book could and should not have found its way into print.

I hereby also express my gratitude to: Dr. Lester De-Koster, Editor of *The Banner,* who, as one of the first readers of a preliminary draft, recommended that I complete the manuscript and present it for publication; Mr. Marlin VanElderen, who sensed the possible significance of this material for various theological traditions; and the William B. Eerdmans Publishing Company for undertaking the publication of this work.

A word of caution: Early in the seventeenth century James Arminius said that it is difficult to avoid dispute when proposing any new thought for discussion within the church. It may be helpful to remember his four observations:

(1) It is difficult to discover truth and avoid error.

(2) Those who err are more likely to be ignorant than malicious.

(3) Those who err may be among the elect.

(4) It is possible that we ourselves are in error.[1]

It is my hope and prayer that the reader will diligently evaluate what I have written in the light of Scripture, and that by means of such study God will lead us into a more obedient and joyous understanding of his written Word.

Neal Punt
Evergreen Park, Illinois

Note: All the texts quoted are from the Revised Standard Version. Occasionally italics are added for emphasis.

[1]Carl Bangs, *Arminius—A Study in the Dutch Reformation* (New York: Abingdon, 1971), p. 276.

CHAPTER I

"All the Descendants of Adam . . . are Saved"

SOME of the most familiar and best-loved verses in the New Testament seem to suggest that *all* persons will find redemption in Jesus Christ. Think of John the Baptist's words as recorded in the Fourth Gospel: "Behold, the Lamb of God, who takes away the sin of the *world*" (John 1:29). Or Jesus' own words, later in the same book: "And I, when I am lifted up from the earth, will draw *all men* to myself" (John 12:32). Or Paul's explanation to the church in Corinth of the benefits of Jesus' resurrection: "For as in Adam all die, so also in Christ shall *all* be made alive" (1 Cor. 15:22).

In this book we shall be looking more closely at these and several other so-called universalistic texts, trying to do justice to what they clearly say while taking into account the whole of Scripture. Christians are often very uncomfortable with these passages. For if you accept the Bible as the written Word of God, and want to interpret it in a manner consistent with itself, these verses create a problem for you. If here the Bible appears to teach that "all men" or "the world" will be redeemed in Christ, there are also places where it is made evident that *not* everyone will be saved.

What is at stake here is not the sort of technical question of doctrine that is important only for theologians. At issue, in Professor Berkouwer's words, "is the eternal lot of mankind . . . a topic laden with the serious urgency of the grace and judgment of God."[1] Such a discussion requires not only our close attention, but also a deep sense of reverence. The message of salvation is at the

---

[1]G. C. Berkouwer, *The Return of Christ,* tr. J. van Oosterom (Grand Rapids: Eerdmans, 1972), p. 396.

1

very heart of the gospel; and what one believes about it will have far-reaching implications. (A number of these we shall touch on specifically in Chapter XII.) So it comes as no surprise that throughout the history of Christian thought there have been many attempts to interpret the "universalistic" passages in a way that solves the apparent discrepancy between them and other texts of Scripture.

Already in the third century Origen and others claimed that the good news of the gospel is that all the descendants of Adam are saved. They understood the passages we have referred to as meaning that every person, without exception, will find salvation in Christ and that God's judgment against sin is temporary, designed to teach us to hate evil and flee to Christ as Savior. The teaching that all will find salvation in Christ, either in this life or in a future existence, is called absolute universalism. It has surfaced at times throughout the history of the church and has grown in popularity in liberal Christian theology during the last fifty years.[2]

In contrast to the doctrine of Origen, the church has commonly understood the Bible to teach that all the descendants of Adam are lost. Christian theologians have consequently tried to learn from the pages of Scripture who are the exceptions to this premise. The history of theology can be seen in terms of how theologians have defined these "exceptions," those who will be saved.

The pious fourth-century monk Pelagius, concerned that Christians were becoming lax, taught that all are lost except those who by their own strength and determination of will lead a good life of obedience to the law of God, following the example of Christ. Augustine recognized in Pelagianism an unacceptable works-righteousness. He taught that all are lost except those whom God in his eternal, sovereign, incomprehensible love has chosen to bring to salvation. A middle position between these two was that of the semi-Pelagianists. They viewed Augustine's doctrine of eternal election as too severe, and proposed in turn that

---

[2]For a concise yet thorough survey of the views held by leading exponents of absolute universalism, see Richard J. Bauckham, "Universalism: A Historical Survey," *Themelios*, IV (Jan. 1979), 48-54. Bauckham reviews the teachings of Origen, Schleiermacher, Samuel Cox, F. W. Farrar, and the more recent writings of J. A. T. Robinson and John Hick.

all are lost except those who by their own sovereign decision accept God's gracious offer of salvation.

In the church of the Middle Ages a new concept of the way of salvation gradually developed: that all are lost except those who continue to live in obedient fellowship with the church. Over against this the Reformers of the sixteenth century placed emphasis on the need for a personal commitment of faith. In general, the Protestant view of what Scripture teaches on this score is that all are lost except those who believe.

Within Protestant thought since the Reformation, several theological traditions have grown up. Lutherans, Calvinists, and Arminians have sought in their distinctive ways to define further how we come to a saving knowledge of Jesus Christ. Although they differ in certain particulars, each of these traditions continues to teach that all are lost except those who believe. It is important to recognize that most Christians have their understanding of Scripture deeply rooted in one or in a combination of these theological formulations. How one reads the "all," "all men," and "world" passages of Scripture is influenced, often more than is realized, by that theological background.

Since there has been and still is widespread agreement that *not* all are saved, a certain protectionist attitude can be found in every evangelical theological tradition, which never permits the Bible to make the simple declaration "All people are saved." Whenever the Bible does speak of the blessing of eternal salvation in terms of "all," "all men," or "the world," believers have felt compelled to dig deeply for a way to interpret these passages restrictively. Is this the only way out of the problem for those who wish to avoid absolute universalism? Does the fact that not all are saved mean that one must approach these passages with the prior understanding that all are lost and look only for "the exceptions" in Scripture? Is there any sense in which these texts can be accepted as saying that all are saved?

Let me illustrate the problem more precisely. One alternative which has appealed to many devout and competent Arminian and Lutheran theologians over the years is the view that since these texts clearly talk about something which has been done for all people—each and every one who has ever lived or will ever live —they cannot refer to realized or actual salvation but must mean only potential or possible salvation. Throughout the same years equally devout and competent scholars in the Reformed tradition have countered that these passages unmistakably speak of a *realized* salvation, not merely of a potential or possible salvation, so that we cannot understand "all" in the "distributive" sense of "each and every one."

Some questions must now be asked. Do those who wish to do justice to the whole truth of Scripture face a real or an imaginary dilemma when they are called on to interpret the "universalistic" texts? Is it true that the teaching of Scripture in its entirety forces one to deny either the universal element ("all men") or the realized salvation aspect ("are saved") of these passages? Do the "universalistic" passages not mean what they so massively and transparently seem to be saying? Must these passages be interpreted restrictively in order to preserve the clear biblical teaching of particularity in the matter of the appropriation and enjoyment of salvation? I hope some answers to these and similar questions will emerge from this study.

The apparent difficulty, I believe, stems from an assumption common to all mainstream historic theological traditions. This assumption is so basic, so generally held, and so venerable in Christian thought that it seems almost insolent to question it. One can glimpse this elusive presupposition by asking which of the following two statements reflects the Bible's teaching: (1) All persons are outside of Christ except those who the Bible declares will be saved; (2) all persons are elect in Christ except those who the Bible declares will be lost.

Nearly all theological discussion and ordinary conversation operates with the former presupposition — that all are lost except those the Bible declares will be saved. Each tradition sets forth its particular teachings about God, man, sin, Christ, regeneration, faith, atonement, and the work of the Holy Spirit. From its own systematic arrangement of those truths each theology derives its definition of "the exceptions" — those who the Bible declares will be saved — and how they come to the state of salvation. None of these systems of theology begins with the assumption that all are saved or are elect in Christ except those the Bible declares will be lost.

To be sure, it is generally agreed that there are "universal accents" in the gospel. But the prevailing assumption that all are outside of Christ except those who the Bible declares will be saved so distorts these universal accents that universalism is not accepted as an essential and joyous characteristic of God's Word. This unexamined assumption has thus deprived many sincere Christians of the assurance of their salvation and has often placed believers in doubt as to whether they should press the claims of Christ's kingship upon everyone everywhere. It has detracted from the positive, world-embracing, thrilling good news of what God in Christ has done for humanity. It is the positive good news, the universal evangel, that should spur us on to proclaim enthusiastically God's message of salvation worldwide. *All persons are elect in Christ except. . . .*

Although the expressions "elect in Christ" and "are saved" and "those who will ultimately be saved" are not synonymous, they may be used virtually interchangeably for our purposes in this study, to designate those whose salvation has objectively been accomplished by their identity with Christ in his death and resurrection. They are those who will surely come to the fulness of new life in Christ. Their subjective salvation, their regeneration, their new birth and conversion, may take place at any point in time during their earthly life.

The thesis to be developed in this book can be described —in an admittedly oversimplified way—as nothing more than a new way of defining the elect. The elect are *all persons except.* . . . Yes, all persons by God's sovereign grace are united with Christ and will inherit eternal life *except* those who will receive the just judgment of their sins in eternal death. (Precisely who these exceptions are is the subject of Chapter IV.)

Scripture reading is based on certain presuppositions; and we tend to validate our own presuppositions in the way we read Scripture. We should step outside the circle of reasoning which traditional Christianity has used for so long and enter the unfamiliar territory opened up by our second presupposition— that all are elect in Christ except those who the Bible declares will be lost. For many this definition of the elect will undoubtedly be somewhat awkward at first. Because it differs so radically from the traditional understanding, working with it will require an entirely new mind-set. Such an effort will prove worthwhile, however, for with this approach we should be able to appreciate more joyfully the good news of the gospel and respond with greater obedience to the commands of Scripture.

The quotation in our chapter title comes from the great nineteenth-century Princeton theologian Charles Hodge. He accepted our second presupposition, formulating it as follows: "All the descendants of Adam, except those of whom it is expressly revealed that they cannot inherit the kingdom of God, are saved."[3] Or, with the exceptive clause removed: "All the descendants of Adam . . . are saved." Hodge claims that Scripture furnishes us with the premise that *all men are saved,* except those whom the Bible expressly excludes from such union with Christ. This premise he finds in Romans 5:18—"Then as one man's trespass led to condemnation for all men, so one man's act of righteousness leads to acquittal and life for all men."

That this is Hodge's interpretation of Romans 5:18 is demonstrated by his use of this premise to prove the thesis that all who die in infancy are saved. He states: "The Scriptures nowhere exclude any class of infants, baptized or unbaptized, born in Christian or in heathen lands, of believing or unbelieving parents, from the benefits of the redemption of Christ." His argument is that Scripture teaches that all are elect in Christ except those who the Bible declares are excluded. Scripture does not exclude any who die in infancy, and therefore Hodge concludes that all those who die in infancy are elect in Christ.

Two paragraphs later Hodge grounds this premise on the very nature of God:

> Not only, however, does the comparison, which the Apostle makes between Adam and Christ, lead to the conclusion that as all are condemned for the sin of the one, so all are saved by the righteousness of the other, those only excepted whom the Scriptures except; but the principle assumed throughout the whole discussion teaches the same doctrine. That principle is that it is more congenial with the nature of God to bless than to curse, to save than to destroy.

Hodge claims that Romans 5:18 teaches that the work of Christ has counteracted that of Adam in every instance *except* of

---

[3]*Systematic Theology* (New York: Scribners, 1888), I, 26.

those individuals of whom it is expressly revealed in Scripture that they will not share in the benefits of Christ's redemption. Note carefully that Hodge does not say that all persons were united with Christ in his death and resurrection but subsequently some of them were removed from this union. Such a view would contradict the scriptural teaching of the eternal security of those who are "in Christ" as well as John 3:36, which teaches that the wrath of God "rests upon" those who disobey the Son—that is to say, God's wrath *remains* on them, having never been removed. Those who will be ultimately lost were never "elect in Christ."

We must remember throughout this study that both the assumption of traditional theology and the one formulated by Hodge are *working principles.* As working principles, they state a general premise, assumed to be true until, in a particular instance, it becomes evident that we are confronted with one of the exceptions allowed for in the premise. To put this working principle into practice in the Christian life is to view all persons and to treat them as those for whom Christ died, unless and until they give evidence to the contrary. On this basis we are to love all people, share with them the good news of what Christ has done for us, exhort them to repent, believe, and obey, help them, counsel them, and warn them to flee the wrath which is sure to come on all who disregard the witness of God in Christ Jesus our Lord.

Although the presupposition used by Hodge is found in the reference cited, we must go on to note that there is little evidence that he used this premise in the rest of his writings. Even more perplexing is that in the history of the interpretation of the "all" and "every" texts one finds neither this solution developed nor any refutation of it.[4] This perplexing oversight of the view es-

---

[4] The view we shall be developing in this book differs radically from the so-called hypothetical universalism developed by the French Reformed theologian Moïse Amyrauth (1596-1664). Hypothetical universalism (or Amyraldianism) taught that God intended to save all persons and Christ procured salvation for all without exception. This salvation is held in suspension until the condition of faith is met. All persons are naturally able to exercise faith, but the moral willingness to believe is a gift of the Holy Spirit to only the elect. Cf. Brian G. Armstrong, *Calvinism and the Amyraut Heresy* (Madison: Univ. of Wisconsin Press, 1969), pp. 82, 109, 153, 165-70, 177, 183, 189f., 202, 211-14, 266-69, 281. The point of view we shall develop denies any natural human ability to exercise faith. For more on faith as the result or fruit of our union with Christ, rather than a condition of salvation, see Chapter IX below.

poused by Hodge can probably be accounted for by two considerations.

(1) That there could be any sense in which Scripture can say "all persons are saved" has been *unthinkable* for traditional theology ever since the days of Origen. The so-called "universalistic" texts have been approached with a bias which arises out of a concern to refute the teaching of absolute universalism. This concern I consider legitimate: absolute universalism cannot be an option for those who acknowledge the inspiration and authority of Scripture. We plan to demonstrate, however, that although Hodge's premise does full justice to the obvious, direct, simple, and clear declarations of the so-called "universalistic" texts, it does not lead to absolute universalism.

(2) There is much scriptural evidence to establish that all persons are sinners, worthy of the eternal judgment of God. *Being worthy of* eternal judgment is readily equated with *being outside of Christ;* and the assumption is therefore made that the Bible teaches that all persons are outside of Christ except those who the Bible declares will be saved. This line of thought will be explored further in Chapter IV.

Loyalty to Scripture requires us to listen without theological prejudice to all of its message, including the so-called "universalistic" passages. We believe that the premise formulated by Hodge is the key to the proper understanding of the "all" or "world" texts — Romans 5:18 as well as many others. We shall use the term "biblical universalism" for the teaching that all persons are elect in Christ except those who the Bible declares will be lost; and we shall no longer use the expression "the so-called 'universalistic' texts."

CHAPTER II

The Starting-Point

IN Chapter I we referred to Hodge's view that the underlying premise of Scripture is that "all men are saved" and the only exceptions to this general premise are the ones given in Scripture. In this chapter we attempt to demonstrate that this claim, which Hodge based on Romans 5:18, is valid.

Romans 5:18 is indeed an appropriate place to begin. The textual problems with it are minor, and its universalistic elements appear in practically every version of the Bible. Its apparent universalism cannot be evaded by claiming translation errors. Bible scholars have always recognized the significance of Romans as a balanced and systematic presentation of essential Christian doctrines. "From the vantage-point given by Romans, the whole landscape of the Bible is open to view, and the broad relation of the parts to the whole becomes plain. The study of Romans is the fittest starting-point for biblical interpretation and theology."[1] Within Romans the analogy between Christ and Adam described in chapter 5 is the focal point of the union between Jesus Christ and those who belong to him. If we can show that Hodge's premise is established by this passage, then, comparing Scripture with Scripture, we can read the universalistic passages without theological bias.

The basic teaching of Paul's comparison between Christ and Adam is that both the "fall" and the "recovery" were done federally, that is, by way of representation. When we see the effect

---

[1] J. I. Packer, *"Fundamentalism" and the Word of God* (Grand Rapids: Eerdmans, 1958), p. 106.

of the act of Christ in relationship to the consequence of the act of Adam, it becomes obvious that the ground of salvation lies completely outside ourselves and is found in Christ alone. Although the parallel has this basic message it cannot be denied that, beginning with verse 12, there are certain subsidiary truths concerning the effect of Adam's disobedience and Christ's obedience. In verse 12 Paul makes the astonishing claim that the deed of one man had a devastating effect on "all men." He offers proof in verses 13 and 14.

Having said at the conclusion of verse 14 that Adam is a type of Christ, Paul does not wish his readers to draw wrong conclusions from this comparison. He shows little regard for literary style. He has begun a comparison in verse 12, but before he completes it he calls attention (vv. 15-17) to those factors which are dissimilar in the analogy between Adam and Christ. Finally, in verses 18 through 21 the apostle summarizes his comparison between Adam and Christ, emphasizing in verse 18 the *extent* factor of the comparison; in verse 19 the *way* factor (the *modus operandi*); and in verses 20 and 21 the *result* or *effect* of the comparison.

Let us read Romans 5:18 again: "Then as one man's trespass led to condemnation for all men, so one man's act of righteousness leads to acquittal and life for all men." Three different routes are traveled by interpreters wishing to avoid the absolute universalism which appears to be taught in this passage. With minor variations these correspond to the three facets of the comparison between Christ and Adam: the attempt is made to deny either the *result*, the *way*, or the *extent* of the analogy as these apply to those associated with Christ.

Those who would deny the *result* claim that the gift which comes to "all men" according to verse 18—"acquittal and life"—is something less than full salvation. They understand this to mean that while all persons, by their union with Adam and his sin, deserve immediate death, they are graciously spared for this present life through the obedience of Christ.

But the benefit of union with Christ ought not to be so impoverished. Since "acquittal" is contrasted to "condemnation," it must connote more than mere existence in this present life. There is no reason to think that this "acquittal" is anything less than the justification portrayed in this entire epistle, namely, the imputed righteousness of Christ.

Romans 5:1 describes justification as that which gives "peace with God." Verse 17 equates it with the "abundance of grace" and the "gift of righteousness." According to verse 19, it is that by which "many will be made righteous." And it is the grace which reigns "through righteousness to eternal life through Jesus Christ our Lord" in verse 21. It is difficult, then, to see how the blessing mentioned in verse 18b could be anything other than full participation in the benefits of Christ's death and resurrection, and virtually all interpreters do accept it as such.

A second attempt to avert absolute universalism centers on the *way* in which "acquittal and life" come to those who are identified with Christ in this text. It is said that the benefits of Christ in verse 18 come to "all men" *by way of* an offer extended to them, but that these benefits are not actually applied to those who are led to "acquittal and life." This view teaches that Christ purchased "acquittal and life" for "all men," and Romans 5:18b does no more than inform "all men" that this salvation is now available to them.

Again, we must turn to the context. Paul is drawing an analogy between two groups of people. He says of those joined to Adam: "they die," "they are condemned," "they were made sinners." Concerning the other group, those joined to Christ, he says: they "receive the abundance of grace and the free gift of righteousness"; they "reign in life," they "will be made righteous." If verse 18 is speaking merely of a possible salvation and an *offering* of acquittal, not of an *actual* acquittal as the consequence of Christ's obedience, then the analogy between those in Adam and those in Christ crumbles. By virtue of union with Adam, we were not merely exposed to the possibility of condemnation: "all men" were "made sinners" by the disobedience of Adam. The parallelism is consistent: by the disobedience of the one, those joined to him were "made sinners," and it follows that "by one man's obedience the many will be made righteous." This is something quite different from saying that "the many will receive the opportunity to be made righteous."

On the above-mentioned view of the way in which we are joined to Christ, the ground and assurance of salvation shifts from

Christ alone and becomes dependent on others. If "acquittal and life" is a potential blessing merely made available to all, and not a realized consequence, then one's salvation depends on one's willingness to accept what is offered. With this distortion of the way factor of the comparison, the federal headship of Christ to "his own" loses its significance. Theologians have spoken of "corporate personality" and "racial solidarity" to help explain the relationship of Adam and Christ to those associated with them. These concepts indicate the way in which "condemnation" and "acquittal and life" are imputed. But if personal willingness to accept what is offered is the instrumental cause of, or an essential prerequisite for, receiving the benefit of Christ's obedience, while no such personal willingness is necessary to receive the consequence of Adam's disobedience, then there is a basic difficulty in applying the analogy drawn between Christ and Adam.

The problem is graphically delineated in these words of Ernest Best:

> In the same way the effects of the free gift of life and righteousness seem on the one hand to operate in all, and yet on the other to require a personal reception. Paul is torn in two conflicting directions; having compared Christ to Adam he is drawn by his conception of racial solidarity to make the effects of Christ's obedience coextensive with the effects of Adam's disobedience; yet his doctrine of faith implies a personal responsibility for reception of Christ's obedience. These two tendencies make for confusion. How are we to give faith a place alongside racial solidarity? It is perhaps possible to say that it is open to men to deny their solidarity with the Messiah (e.g., by denying his Messiahship), and thus to reject the gift given through that solidarity; but Paul does not imply that this denial can be made effective. We can certainly say that there is a potential solidarity of all men with Christ and a real solidarity of all believers with him.[2]

Best's concluding observation is not very realistic, however. Romans 5:18b speaks neither of "a potential solidarity of all men with Christ," nor of a "real solidarity of all believers with him." We cannot avoid the fact that this text speaks of *a real solidarity of all persons with Christ,* just as it speaks of a real solidarity

---

[2]*One Body in Christ* (Grand Rapids: Eerdmans, 1955), p. 37.

of all persons with Adam. In other words, this text appears to teach absolute universalism. Its clear language does not allow one to avoid universalism by claiming that it speaks of a potential salvation which is merely offered to all.

Various forms of Arminianism have distorted the *way* factor in the comparison between Adam and Christ as representatives of mankind. Instead of different ways, this passage speaks of an identical *way* in which the consequences of the work of Adam and the work of Christ are imputed to those who are united with them. Calvinists, on the other hand, have often taken a third route, namely that of denying the *extent* factor of the comparison, in order to prohibit this text from actually meaning that *all men are saved.* To make this third route credible, its advocates claim that the words "in Christ" must be supplied, so that the text reads, ". . . so one man's act of righteousness leads to acquittal and life for all men *in Christ.*" By this addition to the text the import of verse 18b is to inform us that of those who are elect in Christ, all without exception come to "acquittal and life."

No doubt this reformulation expresses a scriptural truth. However, this reformulated truth is in no way germane to the progression of Paul's thought in this context. There is no reason to declare this particular truth at this juncture, for the parallel with Adam neither requires nor suggests such a reformulation. There is not the slightest hint that Paul is concerned to refute the teaching that of all who are "in Adam," some may not be subject to condemnation. It seems apparent that the phrases "condemnation for all men" and "acquittal and life for all men" are parallel and also identical in the scope of their reference.

It is difficult to understand how anyone can say that in this passage Paul "is not seeking to give guidance as to the problem of the extent of the coverage."[3] True, Paul does not view the *extent* factor as a problem. But surely the discussion and amplification of the "all men" in verses 12 through 14 speak to the issue of the "extent of the coverage," and this is restated in verse 18a. In the absence of any compelling reasons for doing otherwise, the parallelism requires that the "all men" in verse 18b be similarly

[3]Leonard Verduin, *Somewhat Less Than God — The Biblical View of Man* (Grand Rapids: Eerdmans, 1970), p. 78.

understood as speaking to the issue of "the extent of the coverage" in relationship to the obedience of Christ.

John Murray states the formidable objection to this equating of "all men" with "all men" in explicit terms: "There is no possibility of escaping the conclusion that, if the apostle meant the apodosis [the second "all men"] to be as embracive in its scope as the protasis [the first "all men"], then the whole human race must eventually attain to eternal life."[4] For many, this would be in itself a compelling reason for not applying the *extent* feature of the analogy to those associated with Christ. But this objection considers both the first and the second "all men" in abstraction from Scripture as a whole. Working with this abstraction, one will necessarily come to the conclusion of absolute universalism. This conclusion is valid only if one considers the universalistic texts in isolation from the truth of Scripture in its entirety. The broader context of Scripture, however, places a limitation on both the first and the second "all men." Therefore it is not legitimate to draw a final conclusion about the "extent-meaning" of Romans 5:18 apart from the broader context of Scripture.

The preceding objection demonstrates that Romans 5:18 and its *immediate context* place no limitation on the universalistic thrust of the second "all men." The only limitation for this text is found in what is called the analogy of Scripture. It is a rule of biblical interpretation that the general teaching of the Bible circumscribes the meaning a particular text may have. Therefore, the general teaching of Scripture rules out absolute universalism for Romans 5:18 because the analogy of Scripture requires an exception to the basic premise that "one man's act of righteousness leads to acquittal and life for all men."

The universal extent factor was not an incidental consideration in Paul's mind when he introduced the analogy between Adam and Christ in verse 12. The "all men" of verse 12 found its roots in what Paul had already said from the beginning of this letter through chapter 3:20. In 5:12-14 he emphasizes the universal extension by noting that death is universal and reigns

---

[4]*The Epistle to the Romans* (New International Commentary on the New Testament) (Grand Rapids: Eerdmans, 1959), I, 202.

even over those who did not have the law and had not sinned after the likeness of Adam.

Furthermore, Paul does not consider the application of this universal extent to those joined to Christ as an error to be avoided. He does not list this extent among those items which are not similar between Adam and Christ, even though he carefully takes note of the dissimilarities between them in the verses 15 through 17. Rather than avoiding the application of the universal extension of those joined with Christ, Paul specifically makes this application, using the identical "all men" expression he has so completely and precisely defined in verses 12-14. With an identical grammatical construction he applies this same "all men" to those who are led "to acquittal and life" as well as to those who are led "to condemnation."

Some argue that Paul's use of the expression "the many" instead of "all men" in verse 19 proves that by "all men" in verse 18 he meant nothing other than "many." If this argument is valid, it would also apply to the first "all men" of verse 18, and would completely contradict the exposition of the first "all men" as found in verses 13 and 14. A more careful appraisal of the situation, however, shows that in verse 19 Paul is recapitulating the *way* of the parallelism, and that is why he there uses an expression which permits the extent factor to recede into the background. The substitution of "the many" for "all men" on stylistic grounds is permissible because "the many" denotes nothing not already involved in the term "all men." But the reverse is not true: "all men" may not be used when the intention is to refer only to "many men."

In conclusion, we should recognize that neither the first nor the second "all men" of Romans 5:18 is used as an absolute universal, meaning all persons, head for head, without any exceptions whatever. Both are under the restriction or limitation imposed on them by the broader context of the whole truth of Scripture.

The obvious exception to the first "all men" is, of course, the man Jesus. He was not "made a sinner" (to use the phrasing of verse 19 to describe those identified with Adam in the fall). According to the Canons of Dort, "All the posterity of Adam, *Christ only excepted,* have derived corruption from their original parent" (III-IV, 2; emphasis added). We *must always* make this one exception and we may make no others because the Bible in its broader context excludes no others from the first "all men."

In an identical way, the second "all men" of verse 18 is not an absolute universal. Scripture speaks of certain individuals who will not share in the ultimate benefits of Christ's obedience (see Chapter IV). They are not among those who are elect in Christ. We may make no other exceptions because the Bible in its broader context excludes no others from the second "all men" of this text.

No unexamined theological presupposition ought to determine our interpretation of this text. Rather this text and others like it ought to be used to formulate our theological positions. It is neither legitimate nor necessary to add the words "in Christ" in order to remove the universal extent feature of this analogy as it applies to the second "all men" of Romans 5:18. The second "all men" can stand as it is, within its immediate context and within the broader context of Scripture, teaching us that *all persons are elect in Christ except those who the Bible declares will be lost.*

CHAPTER III

All are . . . Some are Not

WE referred in Chapter I to what we called a protectionist attitude among some Bible students, which prevents them from saying that there is a sense in which the universalistic texts of the Bible make the simple declaration "all persons are saved." Their concern is that such a statement would necessarily lead to absolute universalism, the view that all persons without any exception will be saved. In the preceding chapter we saw that the statements "all persons are saved" and "all persons are elect in Christ" become suspect when they are made apart from the teaching of Scripture as a whole. The Bible not only asserts in the universalistic texts that all persons are saved; it also clearly teaches that some persons are not saved or not elect in Christ. Immediately the objection arises: you can't have it both ways. You cannot say "all persons are saved" and also say "some persons are not saved."

This objection is often expressed in discussions of Romans 5:18. In the words of one writer, "it is unthinkable to refer justification of life to all men without distinction."[1] Yet, what is alleged to be "unthinkable" is precisely what Paul does! Neither with respect to those who come to condemnation (the old humanity in Adam), nor with respect to those who come to justification of life (the new humanity in Jesus Christ) does he make any distinction. Romans 5:18 and its immediate context *do* refer condemnation to all without distinction and justification of life to all without distinction. That may pose a serious problem for tradi-

---

[1]Herman Ridderbos, *Paul: An Outline of His Theology,* tr. J. R. de Witt (Grand Rapids: Eerdmans, 1975), p. 341.

tional theology, but we cannot dispose of the problem by simply denying what the text says. As we stressed earlier, parallel grammatical construction of this text does not allow us to say that it refers condemnation to all without distinction but not "acquittal and life."

If we begin with the assumption that the Bible can never say that "All persons are saved," then, regardless of how clearly the universalistic passages may say that, we will not accept or try to understand their message. True, the two statements "All are saved" and "Some are not saved" appear mutually exclusive. But before we allow logic to muzzle the biblical text we should listen patiently and carefully to everything the biblical data reveal about the matter in question.

Therefore, when listening to Romans 5:18, we should not deny that Paul refers justification of life to all without distinction. Our responsibility is to face this question: Since Paul does in this verse refer justification of life to all without distinction, what does he mean, given the overall teaching and the general framework of Scripture? This was Hodge's position, as we discussed in the preceding chapters. His answer is that Paul in Romans 5:18 furnishes us with the basic premise that "all the descendants of Adam . . . are saved," but at the same time we learn from other Scripture passages that there are exceptions to this statement.

Liberal theology has generally advocated absolute universalism (the teaching that all persons—distributively, head for head—without exception come to salvation either in this life or in a future existence) by disregarding the declarations of Scripture that some persons are lost. Orthodox theology denies absolute universalism by reinterpreting the declarations of Scripture that all are saved. Biblical universalism contends that the only view of the universalistic sections of Scripture which neither requires a reinterpretation of those passages nor disregards the scriptural declarations that some are lost is to see these universalistic texts as declaring that all are elect in Christ, and the broader context of Scripture as making it obvious that there are exceptions to this generalization.

There have been other attempts to resolve the uncomfortable juxtaposition of "all are" and "some are not." The claim has been made that such words as "all," "world," and "everyone," refer to "race-salvation." That is to say, even though some individual members are not saved, the organic unit called the "human race" or "humanity" is ultimately saved in God's redemption plan.

A more recent attempt to hold these concepts in proper tension is to say that human nature as it is shared by all persons has been redeemed. "The nature of all men is the same. Jesus did not take the nature of some men and redeem that, but he took the nature common to all men and redeemed that."[2] The conclusion is then drawn that because human nature has been redeemed all persons are now free in Christ to accept the blessing of salvation when it is offered to them in the gospel. However, not all persons do accept this blessing.

The difficulty with such interpretations is that "human race," "human nature," "humanity," and similar terms are abstractions which exist only in the realm of thought. Although it can be said that human nature will continue to exist in eternity, it is not true that human nature was the object of the atonement. Suppose a severe famine threatens the extinction of human life in a particular place. Relief efforts cannot be directed toward the abstract concept of the "human race," "human nature," or "mankind" which exists there. Food and medical attention can be provided only to people — either all of them or some of them. One cannot feed or provide for the "human nature" which is common to the people of that area without actually feeding and providing for a definite number of those people.

Similarly, it is not possible to make "human race" or "human nature" or "mankind" the object of redemption in Christ. Such abstractions are not capable of sin, nor can they be restored from its effects. The fall of Adam involved all persons as distinct individuals — *"many* were made sinners" (Rom. 5:19). So also Jesus came into the world to save sinners, individual persons who are part of God's creation and who by their union with Christ are restored to righteousness. What is united with Adam in his disobedience is not an abstract concept of human nature; and what is joined to Christ in his obedience is not an abstract human nature but a definite number of people.

Biblical universalism understands, in distinction from the

[2]Robert D. Brinsmead, "The Legal and Moral Aspects of Salvation," *Present Truth*, V (Sept. 1976), 13.

above-mentioned views, that all persons distributively, head for head, are saved in Christ as they perished in Adam *except those* — and *those only* — of whom we read in Scripture that they shall not inherit the kingdom of heaven.

Some may wonder whether it is even possible that there be exceptions to universal statements found in Scripture. Does this not mean that the Bible contradicts itself? But the Bible frequently does make universal declarations to which there are exceptions. This is the key to a proper understanding of the universalistic texts.

Consider the following: 1 Corinthians 15:27a says, "For God has put all things in subjection under his feet." When the author of Hebrews used this same quotation from Psalm 8, a qualifying sentence was even added, underscoring its universalistic thrust: "Now in putting everything in subjection to him, he left nothing outside his control" (2:8). But from the time Psalm 8 was written until Paul wrote 1 Corinthians, there *was* an exception to this universal declaration, which should have been understood from the broader context of Scripture. This exception is made explicit in 1 Corinthians 15:27b: "But when it says, 'All things are put in subjection under him,' it is plain that he is excepted who put all things under him."

We can use a parallel to 1 Corinthians 15:27 in order to express the concept of biblical universalism: "The Bible says that all persons are elect in Christ. But when it says that all persons are elect in Christ, it is plain that those are excepted of whom the Bible says they shall not inherit the kingdom of heaven."

Again, we read in 1 Corinthians 15:22, 23: "So also in Christ shall all be made alive. But each in his own order: Christ the first fruits, then at his coming those who belong to Christ." Most students of Scripture agree that the phrase "shall all be made alive," includes the physical resurrection of all believers. Here we have the declaration, then, that all believers shall be resurrected "at his coming." There is no hint of any exception. Nevertheless, "it is plain" from the broader context of Scripture that there are exceptions to this universal statement (see 1 Thess. 4:16, 17).

Other examples may be cited. "All things are lawful for me," Paul writes (1 Cor. 6:12), though surely he could have thought of exceptions. Jesus told the disciples, "With God all things are possible" (Matt. 19:26); yet elsewhere Scripture tells us that God "cannot deny himself" (2 Tim. 2:13). The twelve who were present with Jesus were told that they would "sit on twelve thrones, judging the twelve tribes of Israel" (Matt. 19:28). An exception, we learn later, is Judas. Prayers should be made "for all men," according to 1 Timothy 2:1, but surely not for the dead and possibly not for some others (1 John 5:16). "Death spread to all men because *all men* sinned" (Rom. 5:12); nevertheless, there is one man who "committed no sin" (1 Pet. 2:22).

These universal declarations, like many others which could be cited, demonstrate that there can be exceptions to the universal declarations or generalizations made in Scripture. What we must not overlook is that each of these generalizations points to a corresponding reality. God *did* put all things in subjection under Christ's feet. The basic truth is that all believers *shall* be made alive "at his coming." All things *were* lawful for Paul. With God all things *are* possible. The twelve disciples *will* sit on twelve thrones. We *are* exhorted to pray for all persons. It *is* true that all have sinned and come short of the glory of God.

Whatever the Bible says, it says from within its entire context. When the universalistic texts declare that all persons are elect in Christ, this is never to be taken apart from the exceptions found in the broader context of Scripture. And although there are exceptions and the Bible does make them known, these exceptions do not negate the underlying premise given to us in the universalistic passages, that all persons are elect in Christ. The Bible does make the seemingly mutually exclusive statements found at the head of this chapter.

*   *   *   *   *

Beginning with the premise that all persons are elect in Christ, our primary concern in the next chapter, "The Exceptions," will be to discover whom Scripture expressly excludes from this generalization. All the biblical passages describing those who will be lost are reviewed. One of the questions we shall consider is whether those who have never heard the gospel are among the elect in Christ or the lost. Another is whether the majority of people will be saved or lost.

The key to the validity of the thesis proposed in this study is the interpretation of the several universalistic texts found in Scripture. These we shall investigate in Chapters V and VI.

Every orthodox evangelical tradition is *particularistic* in the sense of confessing that not all will be saved. Is it God or the person who decides whether anyone is to be saved? Did Christ die for any who will not be saved? The answer to the question of why some people are saved and not others has precise limits, imposed by Scripture. In Chapter VII ("Biblical Particularism") we will explore these limits.

Chapter VIII observes that there is one written Word of God addressed to all persons. That Word demands from all repentance, faith, and joyful obedience on the basis of what Christ has done for them. Can these demands have validity and appeal for all people if Christ did not actually die for everyone?

"What Faith Cannot Do" (Chapter IX) is the one thing that it is most frequently acclaimed as being able to do. Faith cannot save sinners. Jesus saves. Nothing and no one else can do so. Why then does the Bible present such an urgent, essential, call to faith? That is the question this chapter addresses.

What significance is there to being a member of the church, the body of believers, if all persons are assumed to be elect in Christ? Must we also assume that all people are to be recognized as members of the church unless and until we have reason to come to the opposite conclusion? Chapter X outlines the boundaries of the institutional church.

Chapter XI speaks of the salvation of all who die in infancy. Much more than sentiment is required to establish this teaching, and a trustworthy foundation for the doctrine of "infant salvation" can be found in biblical universalism.

If the concept of biblical universalism is valid, it will have some far-reaching implications. In Chapter XII we present a few of these as illustrations.

The concluding chapter highlights a discussion of the "all men" passages which took place in one denomination. The issues raised were never resolved because the whole debate was based on the premise that all persons are outside of Christ except those who the Bible declares will be saved. The final chapter then concludes by showing the relevance of biblical universalism for preaching and evangelism.

CHAPTER IV

The Exceptions

THE Bible teaches that, by reason of their real solidarity with Adam, the federal head of the whole human race, all persons are born in sin. They are all sinners, under the sentence of condemnation and death. Such passages as Romans 5:12-14 and 18-19 teach the universality of sin. By reason of original as well as actual sin all persons are constituted sinners and are worthy of divine judgment. Everyone is liable for his or her sinful nature as well as for sinful actions, and therefore by the just judgment of God everyone is declared worthy of eternal death.[1] Human blameworthiness is taught so consistently throughout Scripture that all of orthodox Christianity confesses it.

This truth of Scripture has uncritically filtered into our thoughts and theology as though it were evidence that all persons are *outside of Christ*. Such an erroneous deduction from the doctrine of original sin accounts in large measure for the widespread and firmly held assumption that all persons are outside of Christ except those who the Bible declares will be saved.

It is easy to understand that there is a vast difference between being under the sentence of death and the actual implementation of that sentence. It is one thing to say that all persons, elect and non-elect, infants and adults, Gentiles and Jews, those under the law and those not under the law, believers and unbelievers, are by nature children of wrath and *worthy of* eternal death. It is something quite different to say that all of them *will*

---

[1]See Job 25:4; Pss. 51:5; 130:3; Eccl. 7:20; Isa. 53:6; 64:6; Rom. 3:10-12, 23; 14:23; Gal. 3:22; Eph. 2:3; 1 John 5:19.

actually suffer eternal death. All are worthy of death because "all have sinned and fall short of the glory of God" (Rom. 3:23). However, to say that all are worthy of death is not to say that all are outside of Christ.

In Scripture God's temporary rejection of both individuals and nations was invariably the result of sin and disobedience in a specific historical setting. The same cause-and-effect relationship is evident in every passage of Scripture which speaks of the reason for one's eternal separation from the presence of God, that is, for one's being *outside of Christ.* All people are liable for and polluted by the imputed sin of Adam. But nowhere in all of Scripture do we read — nor is it implied, nor is it to be inferred — that anyone suffers eternal wrath because of original sin apart from actual, personal, conscious sin. Salvation is by grace; damnation is by works — works that persons have done in disobedience to God's law, which they know but wilfully reject (Rom. 6:23). The revealed basis for the execution of eternal judgment is always a personal, individualized refusal to walk in obedience to God's law.

In what follows I have sought to list every passage of Scripture which speaks of eternal punishment as being fulfilled. Some of these texts indicate that the degree of punishment is determined by works, others simply mention works as the ground or basis of final rejection. In either case Scripture teaches that the actual carrying out of the sentence of eternal death is invariably done on the basis of works — actual sins.

(1) **Texts which speak of the degree of penalty as based on works:**

Matt. 16:27—*". . . and then he will repay every man for what he has done."*

2 Cor. 5:10—*"For we must all appear before the judgment seat of Christ, so that each one may receive good or evil, according to what he has done in the body."*

Gal. 6:7—*". . . for whatever a man sows, that he will also reap."*

Col. 3:25—*"For the wrongdoer will be paid back for the wrong he has done, and there is no partiality."*

Rev. 20:12, 13—*"And the dead were judged by what was written in the books, by what they had done. And the sea gave up the dead in it, Death and Hades gave up the dead in them, and all were judged by what they had done."*

Rev. 22:12—*"Behold, I am coming soon, bringing my recompense, to repay every one for what he has done."*

(2) Texts which declare that works (actual sins) are the ground or standard by which the sentence of God's wrath is actually carried out:

Matt. 7:23—*"And then will I declare to them, 'I never knew you; depart from me, you evildoers.' "*

Matt. 25:42, 45—*". . . for I was hungry and you gave me no food. . . . 'Truly, I say to you, as you did it not to one of the least of these, you did it not to me.' "*

John 3:36b—*"He who does not obey the Son shall not see life, but the wrath of God rests upon him."*

John 5:29b—*". . . and those who have done evil, to the resurrection of judgment."*

Rom. 1:20b—*"So they are without excuse."*

Rom. 1:24, 25—*"Therefore God gave them up. . . , because they exchanged the truth about God for a lie."*

Rom. 1:26a—*"For this reason God gave them up to dishonorable passions."*

Rom. 1:28—*"And since they did not see fit to acknowledge God, God gave them up to a base mind. . . ."*

Rom. 2:1, 2—*"Therefore you have no excuse, O man, whoever you are, when you judge another; for in passing judgment upon him you condemn yourself, because you, the judge, are doing the very same things. We know that the judgment of God rightly falls upon those who do such things."*

Rom. 2:5-8—*"But by your hard and impenitent heart you are storing up wrath for yourself on the day of wrath when God's righteous judgment will be revealed. For he will render to every man according to his works: to those who by patience in well-doing seek for glory and honor and immortality, he will give* *eternal life; but for those who are factious and do not obey the truth, but obey wickedness, there will be wrath and fury."*

1 Cor. 6:9b, 10—*"Do not be deceived; neither the immoral, nor idolaters, nor adulterers, nor sexual perverts, nor thieves, nor the greedy, nor drunkards, nor revilers, nor robbers will inherit the kingdom of God."*

Eph. 5:5, 6—*"Be sure of this, that no fornicator or impure man, or one who is covetous (that is, an idolater), has any inheritance in the kingdom of Christ and of God. Let no one deceive you with empty words, for it is because of these things that the wrath of God comes upon the sons of disobedience."*

2 Thess. 2:12—*". . . so that all may be condemned who did not believe the truth but had pleasure in unrighteousness."*

Rev. 22:15—*"Outside are the dogs and sorcerers and fornicators and murderers and idolaters, and every one who loves and practices falsehood."*

These references do not lead to the conclusion that no one will suffer the consequences of original sin or that the guilt of original sin has been removed for all. All persons are responsible for their sin in Adam as well as for their other transgressions. The only conclusion we can draw on the basis of this scriptural evidence is that God has chosen not to carry out judgment against original sin except on those individuals who have followed their own ways, making their own personal decisions against God. Original sin is never punished apart from the committing of actual sin. Concerning those who are finally lost, it must be said (according to a post-Reformation creed) that God permits each and every one of them "to follow *their own ways,* at last, for the declaration of his justice, to condemn and punish them forever, not only on account of their unbelief, but also for all their other sins" (Canons of Dort, I, 15; emphasis added).

Nor, of course, do we conclude on the basis of the texts cited that all who commit such transgressions will experience God's eternal wrath. Christ Jesus came into the world to save sinners. But the passages do warrant the deduction that those who will be finally lost are condemned because they committed such sins. Each of these receives a just judgment according "to what he has done in the body."

Can "the exceptions" — those who will be lost — be defined as all and only those who persistently and ultimately refuse to respond to the call of the gospel? This question arises within Lutheran theology. Lutheranism teaches that the effectual gospel call reaches all who live, even though, as Heinrich Schmid concedes, "the proof that the call has reached all nations and all individuals . . . is not easy for us to produce."[2]

Lutheran theology also takes the next logical step: from the teaching that no one is saved without the means of grace (primarily the preached Word) the conclusion is drawn that neither are any lost except those who reject the effectual gospel call. However, the passages which establish the basis on which the sentence of eternal punishment is passed do not limit the cause of such condemnation to rejection of the gospel call. Ultimate separation from God's presence is attributable to disobedience to the will of God as it has been made known to humankind in special or natural revelation (Rom. 1 and 2).

This disobedience or failure to honor God's will is not limited to an intellectual denial of what God has made known concerning himself. Unbelief is expressed in every violation of the law of God — as it is written on human hearts (Rom. 2:15) or found in the gospel of Jesus Christ (Rom. 2:16). Just as obedience is inseparably joined to faith and is essential to it (1 John 2:4), so disobedience finds its origin in unbelief and is ultimately accounted for by it — a disregard of God and his will.

Disregard of God's will can be expressed not only in doing what is contrary to it; it can also be evidenced in doing nothing.

---

[2]Heinrich Schmid, *The Doctrinal Theology of the Evangelical Lutheran Church*, tr. C. A. Hay and H. E. Jacobs (Philadelphia: Lutheran Publication Society, 1889), p. 449. On pp. 448ff. Schmid quotes John F. Koenig, John A. Quenstedt, David Hollaz, and others to the effect that either directly or indirectly the gospel reaches all persons. Indirectly, in that (1) there were three times in which God caused the "news of salvation" to be proclaimed to all living persons — the days of Adam, of Noah, and the Apostles. This news was passed from generation to generation. (2) General revelation as well as rumor concerning a people who worship the true God are invitations and excitements to lead those living far off to seek the gates of the church. Not to respond to these invitations is to reject the gospel call.

Those who stand before the express will of God for their lives and choose to ignore what has been made known to them or to remain insensible to the claims made on them are not without guilt for their indifference. The apostle James speaks of this: "Whoever knows what is right to do and fails to do it, for him it is sin" (James 4:17).

That the ultimate judgment of separation from God is actually carried out only on those who have chosen to disregard God by their unbelief and other acts of disobedience is obviously compatible with the premise that all are elect in Christ except those who the Bible declares will be lost. One may wonder about the validity of this premise, however, in view not only of the Bible's warning to us to refrain from certain deeds lest we be lost but also its exhortation to do certain things in order that we may be saved.

Those who would be saved must "believe," "repent," "obey," "come to Christ," and "follow" him. Are these requirements for enjoying the forgiveness of sins and the riches of eternal life compatible with the premise that "all are elect in Christ except. . . ?" Scripture appears to require certain positive responses of sinners if they are to be joined to Christ and become partakers of salvation. We shall discuss this at length in Chapter IX, where we consider the requirements for and the basis of salvation.

On the basis of the premise of biblical universalism, one might conclude that those who will be saved will be more than those who will be lost. It is true that this premise presupposes a definite number of elect, but it does not address the issue of the relative number of saved versus those ultimately lost. Nothing is gained by speculating about "few" or "many." Jesus himself refused to be drawn into a discussion about this (Luke 13:23-30). Nowhere does Scripture provide an answer to hypothetical questions about the "statistics" of salvation.

Those who maintain that the number of the redeemed is small must reckon with the fact that true believers are said to be the descendants of Abraham (Gal. 3:7, 29) and that "if one can count the dust of the earth, [Abram's] descendants also can be counted" (Gen. 13:16). It should also be remembered that those clothed in white robes in the book of Revelation are described as "a great multitude which no man could number" (Rev. 7:9).

28

What about the kingdom parables told by our Lord? Some of them seem to suggest a small proportion of saved over against the number of those ultimately lost. Each of these parables has a specific, primary lesson to impart, and none of them is intended to satisfy our curiosity about the relative numbers of those who will be lost and those who are ultimately saved. The statement ". . . those who find it are few" (Matt. 7:14) is not a numerical calculation of the extent of the atonement. It is an exhortation: to covet salvation as a rare, invaluable treasure; to forsake all other interests in order to attain the desired end. An attitude of nonchalantly drifting along with a crowd is self-deceptive. The import of "few" finding is identical to that of finding a hidden treasure or pearl of great price (Matt. 15:44-46). The wisdom of a direct, narrow, single-minded pursuit is grounded upon the intrinsic value of the treasure, it is not a declaration of limited accessibility. There is no more reason to conclude from the parable of the Two Ways "that the saved shall be few compared to the lost" than to suppose that the parable of the Ten Virgins teaches that "they shall be precisely equal in number," says Loraine Boettner.[3]

We must also briefly consider what, if anything, biblical universalism would imply concerning the possible salvation of those who have lived their entire life in the non-Christian, pagan world. Our first remark is that we cannot rule out every possibility of their being saved. Boettner speaks to this issue:

> We do not deny that God can save even the adult heathen people if he chooses to do so, for His Spirit works when and where and how he pleases, with means or without means. If any such are saved, however, it is by a miracle of pure grace. Certainly God's ordinary method is to gather His elect from the evangelized portion of mankind, although we must admit the possibility that by an extraordinary method some few of His elect may be gathered from the unevangelized portion.[4]

The *Conclusions of Utrecht* allowed the same possibility in these words:

> Synod does not dispute that God is able also apart from the preaching of the Word — as, for instance, in the pagan world —

[3]*The Reformed Doctrine of Predestination* (Grand Rapids: Eerdmans, 1951), p. 140.
[4]*Ibid.*, p. 119.

to regenerate those whom He will, yet synod judges that on the basis of the Word of God we are not able to make any declaration in respect to the question whether this actually occurs.[5]

To say that many, few, or no such adult pagans will be saved would be venturing beyond the revealed Word. We should leave such hidden things to God. What biblical universalism does teach is that no one rejected on the judgment day will be able to attribute his or her damnation to God, to the union of all of us with Adam in original sin, to the insufficiency of Christ's atonement, or to the fact that the gospel was never presented to him or her. The condemnation of everyone who is lost will be wholly attributable to himself or herself for having disregarded God's revealed will.

The scriptural teaching is that all persons are saved in Christ as they died in Adam except those of whom the Bible says they will not inherit the kingdom of God. There are two categories or classifications of persons who will be eternally separated from the presence of God. "All who have sinned without the law will also perish without the law, and all who have sinned under the law will be judged by the law" (Rom. 2:12). There are those who will be "without excuse" because they did not honor God as he has made himself known "in the things that have been made" (Rom. 1:19-21); and those who "are condemned" because they have "not believed in the name of the only Son of God" (John 3:18).

An uncomplicated and biblically accurate description of "the exceptions" referred to in our premise — all are elect in Christ except those who the Bible declares will be lost — is this: those who do not "see fit to acknowledge God" (Rom. 1:28). Those who will be lost are those, and those only, who wilfully and ultimately refuse to acknowledge God — whether this refusal is expressed in indifference towards, violation of, or lack of conformity to the law (the will) of God as it has been made known to them.

[5]Quoted by Howard Spaan, in *Christian Reformed Church Government* (Grand Rapids: Kregel, 1968), p. 210.

CHAPTER V

A Fresh Approach to the Universalistic Texts

IT is clear from Scripture that not everything God desires or wishes to happen has always happened. For example, "Oh that they had such a mind as this always, to fear me and to keep my commandments, that it might go well with them and their children for ever!" (Deut. 5:29) is an expressed divine desire which has obviously never been fully realized.

So also it is God's desire that all people should turn from their evil ways and live. "For I have no pleasure in the death of any one, says the Lord God; so turn, and live" (Ezek. 18:32). This theme is picked up in the New Testament. God our Savior "desires all men to be saved and to come to the knowledge of the truth" (1 Tim. 2:4), "not wishing that any should perish, but that all should reach repentance" (2 Pet. 3:9). On the basis of these and similar verses Reformed scholars have taught that a sincere offer of salvation is freely extended to all persons, even though God has not decreed the salvation of all. It is conceded that such a universal offer cannot be logically harmonized with a limited number decreed to salvation. Both, however, are maintained because they are found in God's Word.

John Calvin did not believe that ultimately there are two wills in God — a will of desire and a will of determined purpose — but he did say that as an accommodation to our limited understanding Scripture speaks of two seemingly contrary wills.[1] John

---

[1]*Institutes of the Christian Religion*, ed. J. T. McNeill, tr. F. L. Battles (Philadelphia: Westminster, 1960), III, xxiv, 17.

Murray and Ned B. Stonehouse conclude their study on the free offer of the gospel by saying:

> This will of God to repentance and salvation is universalized and reveals to us, therefore, that there is in God a benevolent loving-kindness toward the repentance and salvation of even those whom he has not decreed to save. This pleasure, will, desire is expressed in the universal call to repentance.[2]

Together with God's expressed desire for the salvation of all persons and the universal offer of salvation, the Bible also portrays the death of Christ as having infinite atoning value. If all were to be saved, or even if there were many worlds of people who were to be saved, Christ's sacrifice would not have to be greater. But these scriptural truths are not our concern here. The purpose of this chapter and the following is to demonstrate that there are many texts which speak not only of *a provision for* but also *an application of* salvation to all people, allowing only for the exceptions found in the broader context of Scripture, as we discussed in the preceding chapter.

Before beginning a detailed study of such texts we shall make a few general observations. We shall be referring to these in our subsequent discussion.

OBSERVATION 1 — The universalistic passages should be approached with the assumption that there is a sense in which the Bible can say "all persons are saved" or "all persons are elect in Christ." In Chapter III we argued that we have an obligation, after listening to the universalistic texts, to interpret them in a manner consistent with the entire context of Scripture. One such interpretation is that suggested by Hodge to the effect that these texts indicate that it is the basic teaching of Scripture that "all the descendants of Adam . . . are saved" (Chapter I), and that only Scripture itself may make exceptions to this premise.

The universalism of Scripture is simply and repeatedly proclaimed. Any theology so developed that it finds the universalistic language of Scripture "indigestible" can and should have its

[2]"The Free Offer of the Gospel," in the Minutes of the Fifteenth General Assembly of the Orthodox Presbyterian Church (Philadelphia, 1948), p. 63.

biblical integrity questioned.[3] Besides, an inevitable result of the protectionist attitude which never permits Scripture to declare "all persons are saved" is that the strongest grammatical evidence has to be conceded to the absolute universalists in their interpretation of the "all," "every," and "world" passages of the Bible.

OBSERVATION 2 — The fact that a text and its immediate context speak of the full benefits of salvation in Christ does not necessarily argue against a universal extension of the text, nor does it prove that the passage must be interpreted in a particularistic way. Many have used this type of reasoning — unsuccessfully — in an effort to refute Arminian and Lutheran interpretations of the universalistic texts. These interpretations are faulted as invalid for claiming too much. It is said that "the view that 'Christ died for all' means 'Christ died for all men' proves too much."[4] The argument is that if an interpreter insists on maintaining the universal extension of the texts in question, these passages will say that all persons are actually saved, and such absolute universalism is of course unacceptable.

In this way the Reformed theologian hopes to compel others to accept a particularism not taught in these texts. Quite understandably, Arminians and Lutherans will not deny the universal extension of these texts when biblical word studies and all the accepted rules of interpretation favor the universal extension which they need as a constituent part of their theology.

The real problem for Arminianism and Lutheranism is the fact that these universalistic texts speak of an actual salvation and not merely of a potential or provisional salvation. Therefore the effective theological question to ask is this: Since the texts clearly say "all persons are saved," what possible meaning can this have within the framework of Arminian or Lutheran theology?

Again, we are kept from absolute universalism by the larger context of Scripture, which makes exceptions to the teaching set forth in the universalistic passages.

[3]This is James Daane's description of a certain type of Reformed theology; *The Freedom of God* (Grand Rapids: Eerdmans, 1973), p. 174.

[4]J. Gresham Machen, *God Transcendent and Other Selected Sermons* (Grand Rapids: Eerdmans, 1949), p. 134.

OBSERVATION 3 — Reformed theologians have been quick to say that most of the universalistic passages do no more than reflect that in the history of redemption God's overtures of grace are extended in the New Testament to Gentiles as well as to the Jews. This explanation becomes a convenient way to handle the troublesome expressions "all," "world," and "every."

Certainly, the revelation that Gentiles are included in God's plan of redemption was difficult to learn for those who were rooted in the particularism of the Old Covenant. Many New Testament references speak of the pivotal truth that in Christ "the dividing wall of hostility" (Eph. 2:14) between Jews and Gentiles has been broken down.[5] The inclusion of the Gentiles is proclaimed so obviously in practically every book of the New Testament that we are not dependent on any of the "all" passages in order to be convinced of this amazing historical development.

But even if none of the "all," "every," or "world" texts is *needed* to understand that the Gentiles are included in God's redemption plan it is easy to argue from the context that many of them do refer to both Jews and Gentiles. The fact is that every universalistic text, by virtue of its being universal, does make reference to both Jews and Gentiles. Therefore the mention of Jews and Gentiles in the immediate context of such passages does not in and of itself demonstrate that the author intended merely to make reference to two categories of people and not to "all people" distributively. The use of such terms as "all," "every," "all men" would be, to say the least, a very indirect way of making reference to two categories or classes of people. If nothing more than both groups of people is intended, the preferred expression is "both Jews and Gentiles," and this formulation is indeed employed (see Acts 14:5; 19:10; 20:21; Rom. 3:9; 1 Cor. 1:24).

OBSERVATION 4 — We may not simply rely on the words "all," "all men," "every," or "the world" to resolve the issue of extent. This is generally acknowledged, so it is unnecessary to demonstrate that such terms are often limited by their immediate context. However, it must be kept in mind that the primary meaning of such expressions is universal in scope. We may restrict them

[5]Cf. Matt. 12:21; Luke 2:32; 13:29; John 7:35; Acts 9:15; 10:28; Rom. 3:29; 11:11; 1 Cor. 1:22-24.

only when the immediate context demands such restriction or other teachings of Scripture require such limitation.

The rule is that when the Greek word for "all" (in the plural) is used without the article it refers to a totality. What is said of the totality is to be considered true of each of the component parts individually, unless there is something which modifies such a deduction. The generic use of the adjective "all" (as in "all men") refers to each one in a group, though not with such stress on the individual that there can be no exceptions.[6]

OBSERVATION 5 — Some responsible scholarship contends that the Greek word for "all" can mean "all kinds" or "all classes" (just as the German *alle* can occasionally mean *allerlei)*. A few of the universalistic references mention various classes of individuals in their contexts (for example, John 12:32; 1 Tim. 2:6; Titus 2:11) and thereby seem to prepare the way for interpreting "all" in the sense of "all kinds." However, in no Bible translation has "all" (in the plural) been translated as "all kinds" or "all classes" in these passages. Nor can one find warrant for the use of "all" (in the plural) meaning "all kinds," either as adjective or noun, in Kittel's *Theological Dictionary of the New Testament.* Alexander C. DeJong makes this observation: "*All* in the plural without the article can have various meanings but, seldom, if ever, means all classes, all types or all kinds."[7]

On the basis of word study, then, it may be said that "all" (in the plural) is seldom to be translated "all kinds" or "all classes." But an even more substantial reason for rejecting such an interpretation of "all" in these universalistic passages is that the expression "classes of men" denotes an abstraction which can exist only in one's mind (see p. 19). Such abstractions do not need nor are they capable of receiving "salvation" as it is mentioned in these texts.

To bring these abstractions back into reality, some have contended that the "all men" texts actually refer to "some persons

---

[6]Gerhard Kittel and Gerhard Friedrich, eds., *Theological Dictionary of the New Testament,* tr. Geoffrey Bromiley (Grand Rapids: Eerdmans, 1967), V, 888.

[7]*The Well-Meant Gospel Offer—The Views of H. Hoeksema and K. Schilder* (Franeker, Netherlands: T. Wever, 1954), p. 173.

of all classes." This, however, is so far removed from what these texts actually say that it cannot possibly be a viable interpretation. Neither in Greek nor in English can "some persons of all classes" be designated by "all" or "all persons." Consider how Scripture designates "some persons of all classes" in a non-abstract way (see Acts 2:5; Rev. 5:9; 7:9).

Even if reference to various groups or classes of people is frequently made in the immediate context of the "all" texts, then, it does not necessarily follow that this is what accounts for the "all" and "every" terms, so that the meaning is "all kinds" or "all classes" of men. Indeed, precisely the reverse may be true: since a universally applicable truth is proclaimed by the "all" and "every" expressions, it is applied to the people in the various groups mentioned. It can be demonstrated, for example, that it is the "all" (universally valid truth) of Titus 2:11 which provides the basis or ground for exhorting "older men," "older women," "young women," "younger men," "slaves" (vv. 2-10)—as the "for" at the beginning of verse 11 indicates (see also John 12:32; Rom. 11:32; 1 Tim. 2:6).

The force of the claims and obligations these passages lay on all persons is lost when it is said that the universal truth they proclaim applies only to some people of all classes. The demands, obligations, and authority of Christ's kingship apply to all persons distributively, and allegiance to him is required of all persons whether or not they acknowledge his kingship.

CHAPTER VI

The Universalistic Texts

BEFORE we begin our close look at the universalistic texts in this chapter, we should note the interesting, and perhaps quite significant, fact that, although technical details relating to the original language must be considered, the conclusion arrived at in this chapter is that each of the universalistic texts can be accepted just as it is found in most English translations. The evidence for biblical universalism is readily discerned by reading the commonly accepted translations of the texts involved.

We intend to demonstrate that (1) each of the following texts speaks of the *full benefits of salvation in Christ;* and (2) this salvation *is applied* to all persons. The necessary exceptions to these universal declarations are found in the broader context of Scripture, as we saw in Chapter IV.

> **1 Corinthians 15:22:** *"For as in Adam all die, so also in Christ shall all be made alive."*

Does the phrase "shall all be made alive" refer only to the physical resurrection of the body, making this a declaration of the general resurrection of all persons? Or does this phrase imply newness of life, including the resurrection of the body—that is, eternal salvation—for the elect? I believe it has the latter meaning, for the following reasons:

(1) The words "in Christ" are used. It is true that this expression can be used to include more than the elect: it is used when the redemption of "all things" is spoken of (Col. 1:16, 17; Eph. 1:9, 10). Nowhere in Scripture, however, is the phrase "in

Christ" used to designate any persons who are finally lost. It is impossible for anyone "in Christ" to be lost. "If any one is in Christ, he is a new creation" (2 Cor. 5:17). Those who are made alive "in Christ" are saved.

(2) Similarly, the verb "made alive" is nowhere used of unbelievers. Kittel's authoritative *Theological Dictionary* says of this Greek word: "In the New Testament and post-apostolic fathers [it] always means 'to make alive' in the soteriological [saving] sense."[1]

(3) The theme of the entire fifteenth chapter of 1 Corinthians is the hope of those who are joined to Christ, for they share in his resurrection.

Some have felt bound to say that the text refers to the general resurrection of all persons because they cannot deny that the second "all" here is a distributive universal just as much as the first "all." They say that Paul does speak of the general resurrection of all persons in contrast to the resurrection of believers, since in several verses the phrase "from dead" appears in the original *without* the definite article "the."[2] This they take to be a reference to the dead in general, and they say that when Paul means the resurrection of believers, he uses the expression "from *the* dead" (with the article).

The absence of the article in these verses has, however, been adequately accounted for by Grosheide and others.[3] They make the point that the phrase "from dead" without the article indicates that Christ arose from the realm of death as a quality, not that he left other dead behind.

(4) The final reason for saying that 1 Corinthians 15:22 speaks of the new spiritual and physical life which all the elect receive is that in verse 23 Christ is declared to be the "first fruits" of those who are made alive. They are also "those who belong to Christ." In neither instance can these expressions designate those who will ultimately be lost.

[1]Vol. II, p. 874.
[2]See vv. 12, 13, 15, 16, 20, 29, 30.
[3]*Commentary on the First Epistle to the Corinthians* (New International Commentary on the New Testament) (Grand Rapids: Eerdmans, 1953), p. 363.

That being made alive in Christ is a benefit which the text applies to all persons distributively (each person head for head) can be seen in these considerations:

(1) "All" appears without the article, and unless modified by the context its primary meaning is "all persons distributively" (see Observation 4 in the preceding chapter).

(2) The very structure of the sentence suggests "all" without modifications: not "shall all in Christ be made alive," but "in Christ shall all be made alive." To say that Paul uses this structure in order to maintain the parallel between the first and second parts of the sentence begs the question. If Paul had meant to maintain a parallel structure without having in mind all persons distributively in relationship to Christ, he could have written, "For as all in Adam die, so also shall all in Christ be made alive."

(3) It is generally acknowledged that the first "all" is a distributive referring to all persons universally. It is most unlikely that the identical word used in totally parallel grammatical construction within the same text would have a different denotation, unless there were some notice of an exchange of terms.

These arguments are weighty in themselves, but they are especially impressive because the only way to refute them is to claim that the benefit spoken of is the gift of new life in Christ, so that this second "all" *cannot* be a reference to all persons distributively. This refutation is based on an invalid theological presupposition, namely, that there is no sense in which Scripture can say "all persons are elect in Christ" (see Observation 1 in Chapter V).

1 Corinthians 15:22 depicts salvation in Christ. The words and grammatical structure of the text point to an unrestricted application of this benefit to all persons. An impartial reading of this verse — indeed of this entire chapter — in isolation from the rest of Scripture would lead one to absolute universalism. Nowhere does this chapter mention any who are ultimately lost; indeed, it says plainly that in Christ all persons are made alive.

But as we have stressed repeatedly, this passage, like other universalistic passages, may not be read and interpreted that way, apart from the rest of Scripture. Therefore the conclusion is properly drawn that 1 Corinthians 15:22, within the general context of Scripture as a whole, says that "all persons are elect in Christ except those who the Bible declares will be lost."

> **2 Corinthians 5:14, 15:** *"For the love of Christ controls us, because we are convinced that one has died for all; therefore all have died. And he died for all, that those who live might live no longer for themselves but for him who for their sake died and was raised."*

It would be difficult to deny the universalism of this passage. Not only does the word "all" point in the direction of universalism (see Observation 4); so does the sentence structure. It reads "one has died for all" — a much stronger phrase than, for example, "all in the one have died."

Mention of the "all" for whom Christ died leads some to take this text as teaching Arminian or Lutheran universalism. They contend that the phrase "therefore all have died" means that in the death of Christ the moral and legal barrier preventing the salvation of all persons has been removed. God's judgment and wrath against sin have been taken away. All have died because Christ died for all and atoned for the sin of all. Christ's death was their death, and salvation is now available to all those who by faith are willing to receive it. "Those who live" is a reference to a more restricted number of individuals, namely, those who accept this universal provision in faith.

Others, while they affirm the distributive universalism of the second "all" in verse 14, find it unacceptable to say that Christ merely made salvation possible by his death. Their view is that Paul has come to the understanding (he is "convinced") that "one has died for all": that is, for both Jews and Gentiles — a totality without the article. On this interpretation, the fact that Christ had to die for both Jews and Gentiles caused Paul to understand that the law brought death to all persons distributively: "therefore [the] all have died" (individual application with the article). That is, the realization that all persons are spiritually dead was brought to Paul's consciousness by the fact that Christ died for both Jews and Gentiles. "And he died for all" (for both Jews and Gentiles — same totality without the article) "that those who live" (a more restricted group, namely believers) "should no longer live for themselves but for him who for their sake died and was raised."

Besides seriously questioning the interpretation of "all" as "Jews and Gentiles" (Observation 3), we should note that both the preceding views suffer from the error of claiming that "those who live" is restrictive and refers to a smaller, yet component, part of the "all" for whom Christ died.

> If we were to suppose that the expression "those that live" is restrictive and does not have the same extent as the "all" for whom Christ died, this would bring us into conflict with the explicit affirmations of Paul in Romans 6:5 and 8, to the effect that those who have been planted into the likeness of Christ's death will also be in the likeness of his resurrection and that those who died with him will also live with him. The analogy of Paul's teaching in Romans 6:4-8 must be applied to II Corinthians 5:14, 15. Hence those referred to as "those who live" must have the same extent as those embraced in the preceding clause, "he died for all."[4]

We must view 2 Corinthians 5:14, 15 in its context. The immediate setting discloses that these verses do not constitute a statement of Paul's missionary motivation, as though the meaning were that, since Paul has come to understand that Christ died for all persons, the love he has for Christ constrains him to go out to bring the gospel to all those for whom Christ died. Paul is not talking about his love for Christ; but he is controlled (or "hemmed in on all sides") by Christ's love for him.

In verse 14 Paul is speaking of a controlling power which has changed every aspect of his life, not just his missionary zeal. Indeed, this controlling love was evident in his missionary enthusiasm, but the point is that he would have been similarly controlled by the love of Christ had he been a merchant, a farmer, a teacher, or a lawyer. In the words of Anders Nygren, when

> a man is laid open to the action of God, God's Agape is shed abroad in his heart through the Holy Spirit (Rom. 5:5), and the foundation is thereby laid for the new Spirit-given, Agape life, of which the subject is no longer the man himself, but God,

---

[4]John Murray, *Redemption Accomplished and Applied* (Grand Rapids: Eerdmans, 1955), p. 71. For further substantiation that Scripture teaches that all those who die with Christ also live with him, see Gal. 2:20; Phil. 3:10; Col. 3:1-3; 1 Pet. 4:1, 2.

Christ, God's Agape, God's Spirit. Constrained by the Agape of Christ (II Cor. 5:14), or led by the Spirit (Gal. 5:18), the Christian now carries out God's work, bears the fruit of the Spirit.[5]

Paul's Spirit-filled life after his conversion was so radically different that many thought he was "beside" himself (vs. 13). He even ate and drank differently (1 Cor. 10:31). He knew everyone in a different way (vs. 16). Paul had become a "new creation," so that everything (not just his missionary motivation) had become new (vs. 17). Now he tried to "persuade men" (vs. 11), to cause them to understand this new life-style, but they did not. In verse 11 Paul expresses the hope that since God understands, his fellow Christians will understand too.

Beginning in verse 13 Paul explains his seemingly odd behavior (his new life in Christ). The *content* of this explanation is not so much rational as evangelical, since he declares the revealed truth concerning the actual status of all those joined to Christ: they have died but they also live in Christ. But the *form* of Paul's argument is persuasively logical. Its structure is this: whatever is said of the totality is true of each of the component parts individually, unless there is something which modifies such an application. Paul speaks of the individualized death and the individualized new life of all who are in Christ. The "therefore" and the "that" (= "in order that") in 2 Corinthians 5:14 and 15 indicate that Paul moves on the basis of the first "all" (totality) to the second "all" (individualized application).

"One has died for all" (a totality, without the article), "therefore [the] all have died" (individualized application, with the article). "And he died for all" (same totality, without the article) "that [the living ones] those who live" (individualized application with the article) "might live no longer for themselves but for him who for their sake died and was raised." From the same truth ("one has died for all") Paul draws two opposite conclusions by way of individualized application of the totality. All have died and all live because Christ has died for all.

We have mentioned that Paul is accounting for his own behavior, which his detractors dismissed as very odd. What was being said about Paul also grieved his friends (vv. 11-13), and so

[5]*Agape and Eros*, tr. Philip Watson (London: SPCK, 1957), pp. 132f.

he wants to explain to them the cause of his radically different life-style. He is convinced that he has died and is living a new life in Christ. It is the love which Christ has for him that now moves him to do everything differently.

The apostle indicates that all (the totality) of those for whom Christ died have themselves individually died and also live a new life in Christ. But Paul offers no proof or demonstration that he himself is included in the number of those for whom Christ died or that he is among those who have new life in Christ. This omission is *vital* to the chain of his reasoning, since he wants his readers to understand that *his* different life-style is due to the fact that *he* has died and that *he* is living a new life.

Is Paul himself included? Yes. He is among the "all" for whom "the one" died. The "all" is a distributive universal which necessarily includes Paul, just as it includes all other persons individually. This is a truth of which Paul has become "convinced" (as the "because" of vs. 14 indicates). Paul is arguing from the premise that all persons are in Christ except those who disregard or reject the truth. With this premise Paul needs no evidence to prove that he is among those who died and who have new life — and consequently none is given.

When Paul accounts for the change which had taken place in his life, he reasons on the basis of a premise which must have been taken for granted in the church, namely, all persons are in Christ ("one has died for all"). He sees no need to validate that premise. He states it and uses it as an axiom upon which he bases his conclusion. Paul is sure he is in Christ because all are in Christ, except. . . . His being "in Christ" accounts for the slander that he was "beside" himself.

To the objection that on this line of reasoning practically everyone may claim to be a new creation in Christ, the reply is: indeed everyone may if, in response to the revelation God has given concerning his will for his or her life, he or she can say with Paul, "Wherefore . . . I was not disobedient to the heavenly vision" (Acts 26:19). Such obedience does not merit, nor does it become the effectuating cause of, a new standing with God in Christ. Such obedience is the fruit of the redemption Christ has purchased on the cross for all persons except those who refuse to acknowledge God's will for their lives.

2 Corinthians 5:19: *"In Christ God was reconciling the world to himself, not counting their trespasses against them, and entrusting to us the message of reconciliation."*

That actual, and not merely potential, salvation in Christ is the subject of these words is conveyed by the term "reconciling," and the phrase "not counting their trespasses against them" places this interpretation beyond doubt. "Not counting" trespasses is the same as forgiving them. Reconciliation is the process by which God sets aside his own legitimate and necessary grievance against the sinner by virtue of the work of Christ. Christ assumes the guilt and penalty belonging to the sinner. By this action God can and does receive all those for whom Christ died, without compromising his righteousness, holiness, and truth.

About the universal extension of this reconciliation-forgiveness, we should make a few observations. For one thing, it is untenable to suggest that Paul uses "world" here in the cosmological sense of the whole created universe. The context, as usual, must determine the usage, and the context here indicates that the "world" of humanity is intended. This is seen by the fact that the personal pronouns "them" and "their" have as their antecedent the term "world."

"World," appearing in the Greek without the article, refers to "world" as a totality, in this instance the totality of persons. Whatever is said concerning a totality is true of its constituent parts, if no limiting factor is found in the context (see Observation 4). Not only do we find no limiting factor here, but the plural personal pronouns "them" and "their" indicate that an individualized application of the reconciliation is intended.

Verse 18 is transitional, reflecting that the gospel Paul proclaimed is the same truth on which he based his own assurance of being "in Christ" (vs. 14). It is the fact that "God was in Christ reconciling the world [the totality of persons] to himself." If it were not for the exceptions found elsewhere in Scripture, verse 19 would teach absolute universalism.

1 Timothy 2:6: *". . . who gave himself as a ransom for all."*

This text has to do with Christ's giving himself, and there

is no reason to dispute that it conveys the idea of substitutionary atonement for sin. Because the atonement is said to be for "all," various attempts have been made to avoid interpreting this verse as teaching absolute universalism.

One such attempt consists of those Arminian and Lutheran interpretations which state that Christ paid the price and atoned for the sins of all persons, thereby making salvation possible for all without *actually* redeeming anyone. Yet it is not the simple word "ransom" which is used here, but the compound word "substitute-ransom," indicating that the exchange of one for the other actually took place.

Another approach is to say that in verses 1 and 4 of this chapter the words "all men" and in verse 6 the substantive "all" mean all persons without distinction of race, nationality, or social position, not all persons individually. Appeal is made to the mention in verse 2 of "kings and all who are in high position" and the reference in verse 7 to Paul as a teacher of the Gentiles. Paul, it is said, is warning Timothy against Jewish exclusivism or perhaps the exclusivism of Gnosticism.

But what this proposal overlooks is that *all persons without distinction of race* is still a reference to "all men" distributively. This poses no problem for verses 1 and 4; but if the substantive "all" in verse 6 is not understood somewhat differently, and *all persons without distinction of race* is construed to mean all persons distributively, then only those who teach provisional salvation and absolute universalists can accept the interpretation. At this point some have sought refuge in the unacceptable claim that the simple substantive "all" means "all classes of people" (see Observation 5).

A more recent attempt to escape the apparent absolute universalism of this passage is to assert that Paul is not interested in numbers, groups, classes, or specific individuals at all. The "all men" without the article in verses 1 and 4 is to be taken as an indefinite universal—"anyone at all," "anyone you please." In this construction, then, the "all" of verse 6 implies a universal availability of Christ's ransom. It is available to "anyone at all." The apostle's concern in this passage is to declare that in the actual confrontation of the sinner with the gospel it is God's positive disposition and desire to save the particular sinner whom he confronts with the gospel.[6]

The difficulty with this approach is that in verses 5 and 6 the gospel is not actually being proclaimed — any more than "supplications and prayers" are actually being made in verses 1 through 3. Although this approach does justice to verse 4, which discusses the disposition of God in the function of gospel proclamation, it does not do justice to the meaning of verse 6. Verses 5 and 6 are not speaking of an attitude, disposition, or inclination on God's part in the kerygmatic (proclamation) encounter. These verses declare who Christ is (vs. 5) and what he has in fact done (vs. 6).

It may be true that as a consequence of Christ's having given himself "a substitute-ransom for all," salvation is now available to all in the indefinite universal sense of "anyone at all." But if that is the case, we must learn it from other portions of Scripture, since it is not taught here.

The following interpretations have been given to verse 6:

(1) "He gave himself a substitute-ransom for all, therefore salvation is provided for all persons universally" (Arminian or Lutheran universalism).

(2) "He gave himself a substitute-ransom for all, therefore salvation is available to anyone at all" (indefinite universalism).

(3) "He gave himself a substitute-ransom for all, therefore all persons are saved" (absolute universalism).

(4) "He gave himself a substitute-ransom for all, therefore *all persons are saved except those who the Bible declares will be lost*" (biblical universalism).

The first two conclusions listed cannot be properly drawn from this text. They are garnered from what certain advocates consider the teaching of Scripture as a whole to be. The third conclusion (absolute universalism) is based solidly on what the text says, but it neglects the teaching of Scripture as a whole. It is only the fourth conclusion (biblical universalism) which is based solidly

---

[6]DeJong, *The Well-Meant Gospel Offer*, p. 174.

on what this text says and is consistent with the analogy of Scripture.

> **1 Timothy 4:10:** *"We have our hope set on the living God, who is the Savior of all men, especially of those who believe."*

The interpretation of this text depends largely on the meaning of the word "Savior." In the Old Testament this word is applied not only to God but also to men whom God had appointed to deliver his people from the hands of their enemies (Neh. 9:27). God is also called the Savior of his people because he delivered them from Egypt (Ps. 106:21) and because he had demonstrated his loving care and concern for them (Isa. 63:8). Although God does similar works for other nations, he is never said to be their "savior."

The Bible draws a parallel between the physical deliverance of Israel from the bondage in Egypt and the deliverance of God's people from sin to everlasting life. It is not surprising, therefore, to find in the New Testament a corresponding enrichment of the word "savior." The word is used 24 times in the New Testament, without exception to designate God or the Lord Jesus Christ (as in 1 Tim. 4:10), never to refer to other men.

Realizing that "Savior" refers exclusively to God and Christ in the New Testament, we may ask next whether it is ever used in the sense of a general benefactor, preserver, helper. No doubt God is such a benefactor: he "makes his sun to rise on the evil and on the good, and sends rain on the just and on the unjust" (Matt. 5:45). But does the New Testament ever use the word "Savior" when speaking of God's work of providence and general benevolence?

In 14 of the 24 instances of "Savior" in the New Testament, the immediate context indicates that its meaning is "Savior from sin" — as in 2 Timothy 1:10: "Through the appearing of our Savior Christ Jesus, who abolished death and brought life and immortality to light through the gospel."[7] In nine further instances the context does not speak to the issue, but there is no reason for

---

[7]The same meaning is apparent in Luke 1:47; 2:11; John 4:42; Acts 5:31; 13:23; Eph. 5:23; Phil. 3:20; 1 Tim. 2:3; Titus 2:10, 13; 3:4, 6; 1 John 4:14.

questioning that it means "Savior from sin"—as in 1 Timothy 1:1: "Paul, an apostle of Christ Jesus by the command of God our Savior and of Christ Jesus our hope."[8]

Of the 24 times "Savior" is used in the New Testament, then, the theological content of the word is unquestioned in 23 instances. Why would anyone suggest a different meaning for 1 Timothy 4:10? The answer is that if the word means "Savior from sin" here, the implication of the text is absolute universalism. The traditional Reformed understanding is that in this *one* instance "Savior" means "benefactor and sustainer of earthly life for all men," and the phrase "especially of those who believe" is then understood to indicate that God is the Savior from sin for those who believe.

The general Arminian and Lutheran interpretation is that God is the "Savior of all men" in the sense that he designed to save all persons and so has made provision for their salvation. The qualifying phrase "especially of those who believe" is then seen as a reference to those who accept God's gracious provision in faith. The text, however, says quite plainly that God is "the Savior of all men," and to be their potential Savior or only to have made provision for their salvation would not make God their Savior any more than one who desired and attempted to save a drowning victim could be called the victim's "savior."

Both the traditional Reformed and the "provisional salvation" interpretations place a disjunction between the nature of the salvation which has to do with "all men" and that which has to do with "those who believe." But the word "especially" does not permit such a disjunction. "Especially" speaks of more of the *same*. It does not ever change the essence or the effect of the action to which it refers; it only connotes an intensity or concentration of that action. A review of its other uses in the New Testament confirms this.[9]

Typical of how this word is used is 2 Timothy 4:13: "When you come, bring the cloak that I left with Carpus at Troas, also the books, and above all [especially] the parchments." Paul

---

[8]See also Titus 1:3, 4; 2 Pet. 1:1, 11; 2:20; 3:2, 18; Jude 25.
[9]See Acts 20:38; 25:26; 26:3; Gal. 6:10; Phil. 4:22; 1 Tim. 4:10; 5:8, 17; Titus 1:10; Phm. 16; 2 Pet. 2:10.

surely meant nothing different with regard to the parchments from what he had in mind for the cloak and the books. By the word "especially" he simply meant to tell Timothy to concentrate on, to be particularly aware of, to be alert to taking the same action in respect to the parchments as to the cloak and books.

So 1 Timothy 4:10 teaches that God is "the Savior of all men" (in the biblical universal sense). Some of those referred to may not yet be born, others may have temporarily rejected the gospel, still others may not have heard the good news and will come to a knowledge of Christ as their Savior later in life. "Especially of those who believe" means that believers concentrate on, are aware of, are alert to, are cognizant of the fact that God is their Savior from sin. They know him, love him, serve him, and find all their joy in him.

Titus 2:11: *"For the grace of God has appeared for the salvation of all men."*

The central question here is whether the phrase "all men" should be read with the verb "has appeared" or joined to the word "salvation" (in the original, "saving"). Some say that the issue is in doubt and could be decided either way, but most interpreters agree that the structure of the sentence points to the reading adopted by the Revised Standard Version. This reading, of course, poses a problem for everyone except the absolute universalist and the biblical universalist.

Some Lutheran theologians have preserved the universal element in this text by adopting the minority reading linking "all men" with the verb "has appeared." The problem with that interpretation is explaining in what sense salvation has appeared to all persons, since it is self-evident that there are those who never heard and those who never will hear the gospel. The solution of claiming that all persons are called by the Word of God at least by the "indirect" proclamation of the gospel (see Chapter IV, footnote 2) has not been convincing to all Lutherans. Lutheran historian Lars Nielsen Dahle speculates about a *postmortem* confrontation, concluding that "the gospel, the message of salvation, testimony concerning Christ, must come to everyone before the final judgment can be passed upon him. If it does not reach him in this life, then we see no other conclusion than that it will come to him after death."[10]

Others conclude that Paul intends to say that the grace of God has appeared "saving all classes of men," and they substantiate their contention by noting that various classes of men are mentioned in the immediate context. As noted earlier (see Observation 5) we find this solution unacceptable.

Still others avoid absolute universalism by arbitrarily adding words such as *"capable of bringing* salvation to all," or *"offering* salvation to all," or *"providing* salvation for all." Such additions will be necessary as long as one does not accept the fundamental premise that all persons are elect in Christ except those who the Bible declares will be lost.

> **Hebrews 2:9b:** *"So that by the grace of God he might taste death for every one."*

The only attempt made to limit the universal-substitutionary element in this text is the claim that it refers to the category or kind of persons mentioned in the immediate context — those who are "sons," "brethren" of Christ, and the "sanctified" (see vv. 10, 11). It is said that Christ tasted of death "for every one" in this classification of people.

Grammatically, "every one" has a standing independent of those mentioned in the immediate context, although as a universal term it necessarily includes them. If, however, the author had intended the term "every one" to convey the idea of each individual within the category depicted in the context, he would have used a demonstrative pronoun, so that the translation would read: "so that he might taste death for all *of these."*

Plainly, this text is an individualistic universal, depicting the tasting of death in the place of "every one." The singular form stresses the thought "every *one* individually." Most English versions translate this verse accurately; they use no demonstrative pronoun to restrict this action of Christ to a particular category. Whatever reasons there might be for restricting the text to everyone within a category of people are theological not grammatical.

[10]*Life After Death,* tr. J. Beveridge (Edinburgh: T. & T. Clark, 1896), p. 187.

An accurate translation of this verse is readily agreed on. It cannot be denied that it speaks of Christ as having tasted death "for every one." To do justice to the text, in the light of the teachings of Scripture as a whole, it appears that one is required to choose between two conclusions. Either he "tasted death" (paid the price of sin) "for every one" and therefore some of those for whom Christ paid the price of sin are not ultimately saved (Arminian or Lutheran universalism); or he tasted death "for every one" and therefore all persons are elect in Christ except those who the Bible declares will be lost (biblical universalism).

> **John 3:17:** *"For God sent the Son into the world, not to condemn the world, but that the world might be saved through him."*

> **John 12:47:** *"For I did not come to judge the world but to save the world."*

The term "world" has many different meanings in Scripture, and the context must determine what it means in a given instance. In the light of what is found in other universalistic passages, many of the "world" texts could be readily and meaningfully understood in terms of biblical universalism. However, because they may be open to other interpretations we shall not use them as support for biblical universalism. This is true of such texts as John 3:16; 6:33, 51; and 1 John 4:14. We shall, however, consider John 3:17 and John 12:47, because there is evidence that they can be rightly understood only in terms of biblical universalism.

B. B. Warfield suggested that in the familiar words of John 3:16 "world" may have an ethical connotation, referring to the world of evil, that is, all that which is the contradiction of holiness, goodness, and righteousness.[11] Be that as it may, "world" obviously does not have reference to moral evil in the verse that follows or in John 12:47. These two verses point to Christ's intention to save "the world": surely this is not the world of evil.

[11]*The Savior of the World* (London: Hodder & Stoughton, 1913), p. 118.

The verb "to condemn" or "to judge" (the same word in the Greek), in conjunction with its antonym "to save," is ample evidence that the evangelist is speaking of the world of people. Only human beings can be "judged" or "saved." In William Hendriksen's words, "Salvation, in the fullest sense of the term (deliverance from punishment not only but from sin itself, and bestowal of everlasting life) was what God had in store for the world into which he sent his Son; not condemnation but salvation."[12]

The term "world" in these verses is an undifferentiated totality. As such, whatever is said about it applies to each of its components (see Observation 4). John 3:17 and 12:47 tell us that the Son came into the world in order that the world (of people) should be saved. Listen to Warfield again:

> The elect—they are not the residuum of the great conflagration, the ashes, so to speak, of the burnt-up world, gathered sadly together by the Creator, after the catastrophe is over, that He may make a new and perhaps better beginning with them and build from them, perchance, a new structure, to replace that which has been lost. Nay, they are themselves "the world."[13]

Christ accomplishes his purpose: The world of human beings will not be lost; it will be saved, because all persons are elect in Christ except those who the Bible declares will be lost.

John 12:32: *"And I, when I am lifted up from the earth, will draw all men to myself."*

The meaning of this verse revolves around the expression "will draw." The same term is used in John 6:44: "No one can come to me unless the Father who sent me *draws* him; and I will raise him up at the last day." In this instance it undoubtedly means effectively to bring to salvation. Elsewhere the word "draw" is used to depict physical force. It is helpful to note that in every instance "draw" portrays a power that overcomes the resistance offered.[14]

[12]*New Testament Commentary: Exposition of the Gospel According to John* (Grand Rapids: Baker, 1961), I, 142.
[13]*Op. cit.*, p. 124.
[14]See John 18:10; 21:6, 11; Acts 16:19; 21:30; James 2:6. See also Hendriksen, *op. cit.*, I, 238.

In John 12:32, therefore, there is reference to the *effective* drawing power of the cross of Christ, that is, to salvation. We cannot say that this text teaches only a possible or potential salvation.

To solve the "problem" of this text — that is, to get around the implication that extension is universal — some point to the occasion which prompted Jesus to speak of the drawing power of his death. They maintain that when certain Greeks requested to see Jesus (vs. 21), his response was that by his death he would draw not only Jews to himself but "all classes" of men, including, possibly, those inquiring Greeks. However, as we noted in Observation 5, there is no validity to the claim that the simple substantive "all" (in the plural) can be interpreted to mean "some persons of all classes."

But if that interpretation were grammatically acceptable, it would have made the answer evasive as it related to the Greeks who had come to see Jesus. At most it would have assured them that some of their fellow citizens — some representatives of the class of persons called Greeks — would be drawn to Christ. Whether in fact they would be so drawn would be left entirely in the dark. There is no real joy in the universalism of the gospel if the proclamation is that "some persons of all classes" are saved. That kind of universalism gives assurance of salvation to no one. It proclaims "release" from prison (Luke 4:18) as an accomplished fact — to no one.

A more plausible understanding of Jesus' response to these Greeks is this. He takes note of the fact that Satan, as the prince of this world, had all persons (distributively) under the power of sin. "Now shall the ruler of this world be cast out" (John 12:31). The binding power of sin is to be broken. The cross would overcome the "ruler of this world." "For God has consigned all men to disobedience, that he might have mercy upon all" (Rom. 11:32). The obedience of Christ counteracts the disobedience of Adam (Rom. 5:18) in every instance except in those specifically excluded by the analogy of Scripture.

"And I, when I am lifted up from the earth, will draw all men to myself." This was indeed a relevant and joyous response to the Greeks who were making inquiry. If they did not "see Jesus," or were not "drawn" to Christ, they have only themselves to blame, because the full benefit of Christ's being "lifted up from the earth" is shared by all persons, except those who do "not see fit to acknowledge God" (Rom. 1:28).

> **1 John 2:2:** *"And he is the expiation for our sins, and not for ours only but also for the sins of the whole world."*

> Perhaps no text in Scripture presents more plausible support to the doctrine of universal atonement. . . . The extension of the propitiation to "the whole world" would appear to allow for no other construction than that the propitiation for sins embraces the sins of the whole world. It must be said that the language John uses here would fit in perfectly with the doctrine of universal atonement if Scripture elsewhere demonstrated that to be the biblical doctrine.[15]

Having made this concession, John Murray then proceeds, as do most Reformed scholars, to argue that 1 John 2:2 does not necessarily teach a distributively universal atonement, since there are other reasons the apostle may have had for using the expression "for the whole world." Murray mentions three separate possibilities: (1) to indicate the *scope* of Christ's propitiation — not limited to the immediate circle of disciples, but extending to every nation and kindred and people and tongue; (2) to emphasize the *exclusiveness* of Jesus as the propitiation: there is no other sacrifice for sin; the whole world needs him; (3) to remind his readers of the *perpetuity* of Christ's propitiation: he continues to be the only hope in every age of world history.

Various Reformed scholars have selected one or another of these options. The apostle John, however, did not intend that his readers would be required to select one from many possible meanings. Murray himself appears to favor a combination of all three: "Hence the *scope*, the *exclusiveness*, and the *perpetuity* of the propitiation provided sufficient reason for John to say, 'not for ours only but also for the whole world.' "[16]

We must now ask: How can it be that scope, exclusiveness, and perpetuity are all implied in the expression "the whole world?" The words themselves carry no such diverse a range of meanings. Careful analysis discloses that such inferences are present only when the expression is accepted as a distributively uni-

---

[15]Murray, *Redemption*, p. 72.
[16]*Ibid.*, p. 74.

versal statement. Solely because "the whole world" is a *universal* declaration does it imply that Christ is the propitiation for the sin of all peoples and nations, that Christ's sacrifice is the exclusive provision for payment of sin, and that the atonement is needed in every age of the world's history.

We need not hesitate to accept the distributive universalism of this text, for which the language of John is "perfectly fitted," because the exceptions to this universal declaration are found in the broader context of Scripture, thereby averting absolute universalism.

Can we perhaps say that there is in this text a potential or provisional salvation (a *universalis gratia*) which Christ has obtained for all persons without any exceptions? Expiation or propitiation means appeasement or the cause for turning away wrath. So if it is true that Christ is the cause for turning away wrath for all persons without any exception, then there is no more condemnation for anyone. Any future punishment for sin would be capricious, since God's just wrath would have been satisfied by Christ's sacrifice.

It should also be noted that the conjunction "and" at the beginning of this verse indicates its close association with the preceding context. Thus Jesus Christ is "an advocate with the Father" for all those for whose sins "he is the expiation." Those for whom he is an advocate and those for whom he is the expiation are co-extensive, as Murray points out.[17] Jesus himself is both the lawyer and the evidence for permitting righteous wrath to be turned away from those who deserve it.[18] With such an advocate, who is himself the perfect expiation, the fate of those represented by him cannot be in doubt.

If 1 John 2:2 and other universalistic texts are seen in the light of the entire context of Scripture they can be most readily understood as teaching the premise of biblical universalism — that all persons are elect in Christ except those who the Bible declares will be lost.

---

[17]*Ibid.*, p. 75.

[18]John Owen, *The Death of Death in the Death of Christ* (London: Banner of Truth, 1959), presents biblical evidence to establish that those for whom Christ made oblation are the same individuals for whom he makes intercession (pp. 70-88).

CHAPTER VII

Biblical Particularism

> It would be a mistake to assume that we have to do here only
> with . . . a discussion that was at home in a time gone by when
> ivory tower scholars debated among themselves. . . . The same
> problem is on today's agenda and is tackled with every bit as
> much spirit as it used to be.[1]

IN these words G. C. Berkouwer describes the ongoing debate
about predestination as a live and unsettled theological issue. Similarly, the issue we consider in this chapter, closely related to predestination, is also very relevant: the teaching which in the Calvinistic tradition has come to be known as limited atonement and
which may also be called effective, definite, or (as in this chapter)
particular atonement.

Calvinistic theology has always taught that the atonement
was made for all and only those who were chosen in Christ "before
the foundation of the world" (Eph. 1:4). A typical statement of
this view of the atonement is that of John Murray:

> The atonement was designed for those and for those only who
> are ultimately the beneficiaries of what it is in its proper conno-
> tation. And likewise when we think of Christ's "dying for" in the
> substitutionary terms which are its proper import, we must say
> that he did not die for the non-elect. For it is one thing to say
> that the non-elect are the recipients of many benefits that ac-
> crue from Christ's death; it is something entirely different to say

[1]Berkouwer, *A Half Century of Theology,* tr. L. B. Smedes (Grand
Rapids: Eerdmans, 1977), p. 83.

that they are the partakers or were intended to be partakers of the vicarious substitution which "died for" properly connotes.[2]

Both the advocates and the opponents of this description of particular atonement err when they say that such a view is *necessarily* based on the understanding that election is God's determination from eternity of the ultimate destiny of all persons —a determination which has resulted in the division of humanity into two camps: those elected to salvation and those rejected from the eternal presence of God. Their destiny is said to be equally ultimate in the sense that "ultimately the only explanation of the differentiation is the sovereign will of God."[3]

Those who understand election in this way say that whether one speaks of election as an "election of individuals" or as "a fixed decree" or as "the unchangeable purpose of God," one has to picture a "two-camp" configuration of elect and non-elect. It then makes little difference whether one describes the atonement as particular or in terms of any similar modifiers: any claim that the atonement is effective for all and only the elect must in the nature of the case result in a two-camp motif of predestination.

The arguments assembled by Berkouwer and others against such an understanding of predestination are scripturally sound. The error of such a view of predestination is in saying that the ultimate cause for the existence of *both camps* is the pre-temporal will of God. Scripture indeed teaches that the elect find the ultimate cause of their election in such a sovereign determination by God, but the claim that the non-elect owe their non-election to the will of God cannot be substantiated by Scripture and indeed has many unbiblical implications.[4] If both camps find their ultimate explanation in a pre-temporal decision of God, it follows that it was God's purpose in eternity to reject as well as to save. Then there *must* be unbelievers, and this *must* is rooted in

[2]"The Free Offer of the Gospel and the Extent of the Atonement," *Torch and Trumpet,* XV (March 1965), 22.

[3]John Murray, Review of Berkouwer, *Divine Election,* in *Westminster Theological Journal,* XXIII (Nov. 1960), 46.

[4]Emil Brunner traces the history of the double predestination problem; *The Christian Doctrine of God,* tr. O. Wyon (Philadelphia: Westminster, 1946), pp. 321ff.

God's will. Such a double predestination—that is, an election to salvation and a rejection to damnation from before the foundation of the world—limits the very purpose, design, and essence of the atonement. The "equal ultimacy" view of predestination contradicts the teaching of the Canons of Dort, II, 6: "Whereas many who are called by the gospel do not repent or believe in Christ, but perish in unbelief, this is not owing to any defect or insufficiency in the sacrifice offered by Christ upon the cross, but is *wholly to be imputed to themselves*" (emphasis added).

Leonard Verduin states the case correctly when he says:

> No Calvinist theologian has dared, as he put in the mouth of a given man in the modality of savedness the sentiment, "All of Thee, Lord, and nought of me," to put into the mouth of a given man in the modality of lostness the same words, "All of Thee, Lord, and nought of me." Even the sternest Calvinist at the Synod of Dordt was ready to agree that to make the modality of lostness as much God's work as the modality of savedness was to fall into blasphemy. Surely this is significant. It seems to show that "election," whatever it be, is not precisely the same as "selection." Surely this goes far to show that in the Reformed system "election" and "reprobation" (better called preterition) are not equally ultimate. [5]

The most profound reason for rejecting equal ultimacy, Berkouwer says, is the testimony of John 3:17: "God sent the Son into the world, not to condemn the world, but that the world might be saved through him."[6] This text is representative of the general teaching of Scripture, which allows for only a "one-camp" diagram" of the doctrine of predestination and a "one-camp" theory of the nature and purpose of the atonement. Berkouwer rightly concludes that "the gospel can be understood and preached only if balance, symmetry, and parallelism are excluded."

Insurmountable difficulties arise for those who favor the "two-camp" view of predestination as well as those who oppose it when they accept as an axiom that an eternal election to salvation or a definite number of elect or a fixed decree will necessarily

---

[5]*Somewhat Less Than God*, p. 77.
[6]*Divine Election*, tr. H. Bekker (Grand Rapids: Eerdmans, 1960), p. 202.

result in a parallel or "two-camp" view of predestination. It cannot be denied that, according to the ordinary rules of reason, if there is an election to salvation from before the foundation of the world (whether we view this as a pre-temporal or extra-creaturely act), there must likewise be a corresponding rejection or at least a pre-terition or "passing by" of those not chosen. Scripture, however, draws no such conclusion. The Bible speaks of an eternal election; it does not reveal a corresponding eternal rejection. God's judgment of never-ending exclusion from his presence must be viewed as a response to actual sin committed by those that are rejected, as we saw in Chapter IV, and we should not permit our understanding of reason to conclude that this rejection of some is the inevitable consequence of definite, eternal, particular election of individuals to salvation.

Because the Bible describes those who are outside of Christ mostly in negative terms, it is more accurate to speak of predestination or eternal election in terms of one camp of persons surrounded by "no man's land." It is "no man's land" because no one has a right to be outside of Christ (Matt. 4:10). Those outside can blame no one other than themselves for being there (John 12:48). No one remains there against his own will (John 5:40). No one on earth is hopelessly and helplessly consigned there (Rev. 22:17b). No one is unjustly there (Acts 13:46). No one is there because God wishes or desires him to be there (2 Pet. 3:9). We do not know and Scripture does not tell us why anyone would want to be there or for that matter even how anyone can be there. The Bible speaks of this "no man's land" as an inexplicable darkness, as "the mystery of lawlessness."

Scripture does not explain the ultimate cause of anyone's existence outside the "camp" of the elect. It simply describes the disobedience, the unbelief, and the consequent blameworthiness of those outside of Christ. Christians rightly sing of the grace by which they are saved as amazing, but given the historical reality of Christ's coming into this world to save sinners it is even more amazing that there should be those who continue to live outside the camp of salvation.

Instead of accounting for the fact that some continue to live outside the camp in unbelief, the Bible expresses amazement at human stubbornness in sin. "What more was there to do for my vineyard, that I have not done in it? When I looked for it to yield grapes, why did it yield wild grapes?" (Isa. 5:4). "Why will you die, O house of Israel?" (Ezek. 18:31). "How often would I have gathered your children together as a hen gathers her brood under her wings, and you would not!" (Matt. 23:37). "He marveled because of their unbelief" (Mark 6:6).

The Bible gives no explanation for some persons' wilful and ultimate refusal to acknowledge God. Just as Scripture provides no hint as to how and why sin was able to mar God's perfect creation in the first place, so also all questions concerning the how and why of unbelief and non-election must be dismissed as unanswerable. The ultimate cause of disobedience and unbelief is lost in the irrationality of sin. In spite of Berkouwer's objections, we may have to use Barth's expressions "impossible possibility" or "ontological impossibility" to describe the act of disbelief. When one considers the act of wilful, responsible, ultimate rejection of God's will in conjunction with the biblical teaching of sovereign grace, it does seem appropriate to say that disbelief is an "impossible possibility," without in any way denying the reality of such an act.[7]

As Daane says, "Surely it is enough to explain the damnation or nonsalvation of the lost in terms of their sin and unbelief."[8] Their sin and unbelief, in turn, cannot be explained. Calvin seems to express a similar sentiment. He says that Adam corrupted the pure nature he had received from the Lord, and by his fall he drew all his posterity with him into destruction. Therefore,

> we should contemplate the evident cause of condemnation in the corrupt nature of humanity—which is closer to us—rather than seek a hidden and utterly incomprehensible cause in God's predestination. And let us not be ashamed to submit our understanding to God's boundless wisdom so far as to yield before its many secrets. For, of those things which it is neither given nor lawful to know, ignorance is learned; the craving to know, a kind of madness.[9]

---

[7]Karl Barth, *Church Dogmatics*, IV/3/1, tr. G. W. Bromiley (Edinburgh: T. & T. Clark, 1961), 176ff.

[8]James Daane, "Christ's Atonement and God's Sovereignty," *Reformed Journal*, XV (Apr. 1965), 17.

[9]*Institutes*, III, xxiii, 8.

However, as Fred Klooster points out, "Calvin never allowed this reference to the proximate cause of reprobation (condemnation) to stand by itself. . . . He acknowledged that the ultimate or remote cause of reprobation, as of election, is the sovereign will of God."[10]

It is relatively easy to illustrate that Calvin attributes the ultimate or remote cause of reprobation to God's sovereign will in predestination. But it is more difficult to demonstrate that the passages Calvin appealed to necessarily do establish that Scripture makes known to us the ultimate cause of reprobation. Calvin's own advice cited above should also be applied to the *ultimate cause of reprobation*. We ought not to seek such a "hidden and utterly incomprehensible cause in God's predestination." In this matter we should "not be ashamed to submit our understanding to God's boundless wisdom so far as to yield before its many secrets." Although Calvin did not always follow his own advice, his advice is appropriate, so that our "craving to know" does not prove to be "a kind of madness."

True, in some mysterious, ambiguous way, the reprobation of some also occurs within the broad perspective of God's "definite plan and foreknowledge" (Acts 2:23). But one may well question the biblical validity of the claim made in the Canons of Dort that the reason some do not receive the gift of faith "proceeds from God's eternal decree" or that " it is the express testimony of sacred Scripture" that "others are passed by in the eternal decree" (I, 6, 15).[11]

The more guarded confession which Lutheran theology makes seems closer to the express testimony of Scripture. The *Formula of Concord* expresses the Lutheran teaching as follows:

> The eternal election of God or God's predestination to salvation does not extend over both the godly and the ungodly, but only over the children of God, who have been elected and pre-

[10]*Calvin's Doctrine of Predestination* (Grand Rapids: Baker, 2d ed., 1977), p. 72.

[11]Cf. the request by Harry Boer that his denomination, the Christian Reformed Church, either make an official public statement of the scriptural basis for the doctrine of reprobation or declare that it is no longer binding on the church and its officebearers; *Acts of Synod* of the Christian Reformed Church, 1977, pp. 665-79.

destinated to eternal life "before the foundation of the world was laid," as St. Paul says, "Even as he chose us in him, he destined us in love to be his sons through Jesus Christ" (Eph. 1:4, 5).[12]

Elsewhere this same confession says:

> Thus Paul very carefully distinguishes between the work of God, who alone prepares vessels of honor, and the work of the devil and of man, who, through the instigation of the devil and not of God, has made himself a vessel of dishonor. It is written, "God endured with much patience the vessels of wrath fitted for damnation in order to make known the riches of his glory in the vessels of mercy, which he prepared beforehand for salvation" (Rom. 9:22, 23). The apostle says in unmistakable terms that God "endured the vessels of wrath with much patience." He does not say that God made them vessels of wrath. If that had been his will, he would not have needed any long-suffering. The devil and man himself, and not God, are the cause of their being fitted for damnation. Everything which prepares and fits man for damnation emanates from the devil and man through sin, and in no way from God. Concerning "the vessels of mercy" he says specifically that the Lord himself "has prepared them unto glory." He does not say this of the damned, whom God has not prepared but who have prepared themselves to be vessels of damnation.[13]

The advocacy of a doctrine of eternal election without a corresponding doctrine of eternal reprobation does not in the least diminish the usefulness of the doctrine of election or detract from "its very sweet fruits" as these are set forth by Calvin. He mentions three such fruits: (1) it teaches us to expect salvation solely from God's free mercy; (2) it promotes humility; (3) it gives God the glory.[14]

That Christ's coming into the world creates a division among people (Matt. 10:34-36) does not mean that there are two camps, both of which owe their existence to a determination made by God in eternity. The division is rather between those in the camp whose placement *was determined by God* in eternity, and

---

[12]*The Book of Concord, Formula of Concord,* Solid Declaration 11:5 (Philadelphia: Fortress, 1959), p. 617.

[13]*Ibid.,* Solid Declaration 11:78, pp. 629f.

[14]*Institutes,* III, xxi, 1.

those outside, concerning whose placement the Scripture tells us only that *it is of their own doing.*

The analogy of one camp surrounded by "no man's land" breaks down at a certain point. There is no physical barrier or externally observable mark to separate the elect from the non-elect. Neither those claiming to live within the camp nor those outside it give a consistent and unmistakably clear witness to their real citizenship. In Verduin's words:

> Men in the modality of fallenness do not under magnification look wholly unlike men in the modality of savedness. They live about equally long; they are subject to the same diseases; they respond to the same medicines. Even when examined carefully as to conduct patterns, the picture is by no means unambiguous. The technician who runs the test cannot even be wholly certain as to the category to which a given specimen belongs. Theologically, the difficulty encountered as we seek to classify may be stated in a dictum that, although not specifically theological, does carry a theological truth, the saying, namely, that "there is so much good in the worst of us and so much bad in the best of us. . . ."[15]

Therefore those who profess to inhabit the camp must continually be exhorted to "confirm [their] call and election" (2 Pet. 1:10). Even so there will be many surprises when the intentions of human hearts are revealed (Matt. 25:41-46). Those who appear to be living outside the camp must be continually challenged to lay down their arms and submit freely to the one who rules over the camp. We must appeal to them "by the mercies of God, to present [their] bodies a living sacrifice, holy and acceptable to God" (Rom. 12:1). Failure to do so will prove to be the just cause of their condemnation.

In the sense that it is required of all persons to repent, believe, and live in joyful obedience — in other words, to live as loyal members of the camp — Berkouwer's warning is well taken. He mentions that the doctrine of predestination or eternal election ought never to seduce us into thinking of or dealing with humanity in terms of two separate groups of people, for among other reasons, "the Bible does not present us with two classes of people, but only one, the sinners who are called to salvation. His-

[15]*Somewhat Less Than God,* p. 81.

torically, we could say that the church always drew back from dividing the human race into the selected and the rejected ones."[16] In Chapters VIII, IX, and X we are going to be developing the theme that Scripture comes with the same approach to *all persons*.

If we posit a "one-camp" configuration of predestination or eternal election, can it still be alleged that any atonement characterized as definite or particular must by its very nature or essence account for the exclusion of some people? The claim has been made that "the phrase 'definite atonement' still suggests that there is something about the atonement from which it follows that there have to be some people that perish."[17] Probably no better refutation of this allegation can be found than Warfield's observation:

> The point of insistence in Calvinistic particularism is not that God saves out of the sinful mass of men only one here and there, a few brands snatched from the burning, but that God's method of saving men is to set upon them in his almighty grace, to purchase them to himself by the precious blood of his Son, to visit them in the inmost core of their being by the creative operations of his Spirit, and himself, the Lord God Almighty, to save them. How many, up to the whole human race in all its representatives, God has thus bought and will bring to eternal communion with himself by entering himself into personal communion with them, lies, I say, quite outside the question of particularism. Universalism in this sense of the term [absolute universalism] and particularism are so little inconsistent with one another that it is only the particularist who can logically be this kind of universalist.[18]

An absolute universalist would necessarily have to be a particularist, acknowledging that God has sovereignly determined a definite number to be saved and that the atonement made in their behalf is effectively applied to each of them. Without such a definite, effective atonement it would be possible for some not to be saved. That is, even if all persons without exception were to be saved, the atonement would necessarily be particular in its nature

---

[16]*A Half Century*, p. 95.
[17]H. Pietersma, "Predestination II," *Reformed Journal*, XVII (Jan. 1967), 19.
[18]*The Plan of Salvation* (Grand Rapids: Eerdmans, 1942), p. 98.

or essence. It does not follow from the particularism of the atonement as such that "there have to be some that perish."

Biblical universalism confesses that the atonement is particular in the sense of being effectively applied to all those for whom Christ made his sacrifice. In other words, it accepts as biblical the doctrine that Christ died for and sovereignly brings to salvation all those and only those given him by the Father in the eternal counsel of redemption. We argued before that Christ could not and did not redeem "human nature" in abstraction from redeeming actual people — either some of them or all of them (see p. 19). There is no abstract group, classification, or multitude which is either capable of sin or of being redeemed, apart from actual people who have sinned and have been redeemed. The Son of God did not come into the world to save human nature or a class of individuals or a multitude of people apart from actual sinners. Neither those joined to Adam nor those joined to Christ are an abstraction; they are a definite number of people.

The Lutheran view here must be distinguished from Arminianism, as we will have occasion to notice in more detail in Chapter IX. Nevertheless Lutheranism, like Arminianism, does teach that God's grace makes equal provision of salvation for all persons without exception — a *universalis gratia.* Whatever God has done for the salvation of any one person he has done equally for all persons. "The gospel as the good news that God has provided salvation for all men for Christ's sake is central in Lutheran theology."[19]

Heinrich Schmid collates the thoughts of many Lutheran writers and outlines a teaching called universal atonement or universal redemption. There is a *universal* or *general will* toward fallen people which exhibits itself in preparing the means of redemption for all and effectually offering this redemption to all. The intention of this universal will is to bring all persons equally to salvation. It is also called God's *antecedent* will, inasmuch as it precedes all considerations of the kind of response persons may make to it.

[19]David Scaer, *Getting into the Story of Concord* (St. Louis: Concordia, 1977), p. 85.

The universal will of God is distinguished from the *special* will of God. The special will takes into consideration a person's response to the offer of salvation extended through God's universal will. This special will is therefore also called the *consequent* will, and it is expressed in the fact that it is God's intention and purpose to bring to salvation all those and only those who believe the testimony of divine grace and persevere in this faith until the end of their lives.[20]

B. B. Warfield made the penetrating observation that to universalize the atonement can only be done at the high cost of losing its intrinsic value: "If it does nothing for any man that it does not do for all men why, then, it is obvious that it saves no man; for clearly not all men are saved."[21] The importance of biblical particularism can be appreciated by viewing it in the light of the response of the Reformed churches to the followers of Arminius. A helpful comparison of the two sides is offered by James I. Packer.[22] He introduces the subject of limited atonement or particular redemption by noting:

Arminianism's Declarations:	Calvinism's Responses:
1. Man is never so completely corrupted by sin that he cannot savingly believe the gospel when it is put before him.	1. Fallen man in his natural state lacks all power to believe the gospel and the law despite all external inducements.
2. Man is never so completely controlled by God that he cannot reject the gospel.	2. God's election is a free, sovereign, unconditional choice of sinners, to be redeemed by Christ, given faith, and brought to glory.
3. God's election of those who will be saved is prompted by His foreseeing that they will of their own accord believe.	3. The redeeming work of Christ had as its end and goal the salvation of the elect.
4. Christ's death did not insure the salvation of anyone, for it did not secure the gift of faith; rather it created the possibility of salvation for everyone if they believe.	4. The work of the Holy Spirit in bringing men to faith never fails to achieve its object.

[20]Schmid, *Doctrinal Theology*, pp. 278-97.

[21]Warfield, *The Plan of Salvation*, p. 95.

[22]Introductory essay to John Owen, *The Death of Death in the Death of Christ*, pp. 3, 4.

5. It rests with believers to keep themselves in a state of grace by keeping up their faith; those who fail here fall away and are lost.	5. Believers are kept in faith and grace by the unconquerable power of God until they come to glory.

Because these five responses of Calvinism are a reaction against something, they have a negative cast. The idea may arise that the Calvinistic view of "limited" atonement or "particular" redemption restricts divine mercy. Packer reminds us that these qualifications are used to safeguard the central affirmation of the gospel—"that Christ is a Redeemer who really does redeem."[23] The human being as sinner is absolutely powerless to improve his spiritual lot. It is God who does everything: He "plans, achieves and communicates redemption, calls and keeps, justifies, sanctifies, glorifies." Thus "salvation, first and last, whole and entire, past, present, and future is of the Lord, to whom be glory forever; amen."[24]

Packer also observes that the theology of the "Five Points" gives honor to the power of the cross. God's saving purpose and his accomplishment in the death of his Son were not merely an ineffectual wish, depending on a human act for its fulfilment. The Calvinist confesses that all those for whom Christ died *will be* saved.

> [The Calvinist] insists that the Bible sees the Cross as revealing God's power to save, not His impotence. Christ did not win a hypothetical salvation for hypothetical believers, a mere possibility of salvation for any who might possibly believe, but a real salvation for His own chosen people. . . . The intended effects of His self-offering do in fact follow, just because the Cross was what it was. Its saving power does not depend on faith being added to it; its saving power is such that faith flows from it. The Cross secured the full salvation of all for whom Christ died. "God forbid," therefore, "that I should glory, save in the cross of our Lord Jesus Christ" (Gal. 6:14).
>
> Now the real nature of Calvinistic soteriology becomes plain. It is no artificial oddity, nor a product of over-bold logic. Its central confession, that *God saves sinners,* that *Christ redeemed us by His blood,* is both the witness of the Bible and of the believing heart. The Calvinist . . . thinks and speaks at all times of the sovereign grace of God in the way that every Chris-

[23]*Ibid.,* p. 5.
[24]*Ibid.,* p. 6.

tian does when he pleads for the souls of others, or when he obeys the impulse of worship which rises unbidden within him, prompting him to deny himself all praise and to give all the glory of his salvation to his Savior.[25]

Finally, we should notice how this view of atonement affects gospel proclamation. The popularity of Arminianism (or *universalis gratia*), Packer says, has conditioned our minds to think of the cross as a redemption which does less than redeem; of Christ as a Savior who does less than save; and of faith as the human help God needs to accomplish his purpose.

> As a result, we are no longer free either to believe the biblical gospel or to preach it. We cannot believe it, because our thoughts are caught in the toils of synergism. We are haunted by the Arminian idea that if faith and unbelief are to be responsible acts, they must be independent acts; hence we are not free to believe that we are saved entirely by divine grace through a faith which is itself God's gift and flows to us from Calvary. Instead, we involve ourselves in a bewildering kind of double-think about salvation, telling ourselves one moment that it all depends on God and next moment that it all depends on us. The resultant mental muddle deprives God of much of the glory that we should give Him as author and finisher of our salvation, and ourselves of much of the comfort we might draw from knowing that God is for us.[26]

The "mental muddle" to which Packer refers comes out of a good motivation, but it flounders in poor theology:

> We want to magnify the saving grace of God and the saving power of Christ. So we declare that God's redeeming love extends to every man, and that Christ has died to save every man, and we proclaim that the glory of divine mercy is to be measured by these facts. And then, in order to avoid universalism, we have to depreciate all that we were previously extolling, and to explain that, after all, nothing that God and Christ have done can save us unless we add something to it; the decisive factor . . . is our own believing. . . . This is a hollow anticlimax. But if we start by affirming that God has a saving love for all, and Christ died a saving death for all, and yet balk at becoming universalists, there is nothing else that we can say. And let us be clear on what we have done when we have put the matter in this fash-

[25]*Ibid.*, p. 10.
[26]*Ibid.*, pp. 13, 14.

ion. We have not exalted grace and the Cross; we have cheapened them. We have limited the atonement far more drastically than Calvinism does, for whereas Calvinism asserts that Christ's death, as such, saves all whom it was meant to save, we have denied that Christ's death, as such, is sufficient to save any of them.[27]

It should be noted that, for all his incisive analyses of the differences between Arminianism and Calvinism, Packer does not address himself to the universal emphasis found in Scripture. Obviously, he sees the particularism of Calvinism, with its assured salvation of the elect, as more consistent with the nature of God and his intention for humanity than the provisional salvation of Arminianism, dependent on human response for its realization. The premise of biblical universalism is in agreement with his view of particularism.

However, Packer's insights fall short of discerning that assured salvation must be construed in terms of the universalistic passages of Scripture. As a result he, like other Calvinists, uses certain unhappy expressions, such as: "Christ died to save a certain company of helpless sinners upon whom God had set His free saving love."[28] Although formally accurate, such expressions leave the impression that God has chosen some fortunate souls to salvation and the rest of humanity is bypassed, through no fault of its own. Working with the premise of biblical universalism, one can better say, "Christ died for all persons except certain specified sinners." Those sinners are specified in the Bible as all who wilfully and ultimately refuse to acknowledge God.

We cannot — and need not — present all the evidence for particularism here: it is readily available from other sources.[29] But it is in order to mention the following considerations:

(1) The language Scripture uses to describe the work of

---

[27]*Ibid.*, p. 14.

[28]*Ibid.*, p. 15.

[29]See for example the two books by David N. Steele and Curtis C. Thomas, *Romans: An Interpretive Outline* (esp. pp. 168-75); and *The Five Points of Calvinism: Defined, Defended, Documented* (both Philadelphia: Presbyterian and Reformed, 1963). The biblical foundation for each point is provided, together with a bibliography of works in English. Among the texts cited for particular redemption are Matt. 1:21; 20:28; 26:28; John 10:11; 11:50-53; Acts 20:28; Rom. 8:32-34; Eph. 5:25-27; Heb. 2:17; 3:1; 9:15, 28; Rev. 5:9.

Christ is definitive. Roger R. Nicole mentions three examples: (a) *Redemption,* the gracious action by which our Lord Jesus Christ purchased us in order to liberate us from sin and its consequences. Does redemption truly occur if those who have been redeemed ultimately remain in bondage to sin? (b) *Propitiation,* which describes how the wrath of God against sinners is assuaged by Christ's death. Is it truly propitiation if its beneficiaries forever remain under God's wrath? (c) *Reconciliation.* Is it truly reconciliation if the parties involved forever remain at enmity? The very language of the Bible does not allow us to view the work of Christ as something well-intended but not necessarily effectual. Redemption, propitiation, and reconciliation are accomplished for all who are in Christ.[30]

(2) Many passages of Scripture describe the work of Christ and his motivation, reason, or purpose for performing it. He was to be called Jesus, because he would "save his people from their sins" (Matt. 1:21); he came down from heaven in order that he "should lose nothing of all that" were given him by the Father (John 6:38, 39); he would lay down his life for the sheep in order that "they might have life and have it abundantly" (John 10:10, 11); and he gave himself up "for the church" so that he might present the church to himself "holy and without blemish" (Eph. 5:26, 27).

In addition to the expressed intention, design, goal, plan, and purpose for being called "Jesus," for "coming down from heaven," for "laying down his life," and "giving himself up," Scripture tells us that there are some who will not be "saved from their sins," will be "lost," will never "have life," and will never become "holy and without blemish."

In view of the declared purpose for Jesus' coming into the world it appears we must draw one of two conclusions. Either the Lord Jesus Christ, to whom "all authority in heaven and on earth has been given" for the express purpose of calling and gathering people to salvation (Matt. 28:18), is unsuccessful in accomplishing his intention for all people (Arminian and Lutheran view of the atonement); or those who are ultimately not "saved" were never

[30]Roger R. Nicole, "Particular Redemption," *Tenth: An Evangelical Quarterly* (July 1978), pp. 64f.

included in the saving purpose of Christ's death (Calvinistic view of the atonement).

(3) The chain of events involving redemption, as Romans 8:29, 30 depicts it, cannot be broken. Whether the "links" in this chain are arranged in a significant temporal sequence is not germane here. The point is that there is an unbreakable connection between the various aspects of the way of salvation. One cannot claim that Murray would accept biblical universalism's definition of the "us" of verse 31 as all persons except those who the Bible declares will be lost; nevertheless, he has clearly demonstrated that the "us" of Romans 8:39 denotes all those and only those spoken of as the ones "whom he foreknew" in Romans 8:29.[31] All those whom Christ "foreknew," without any exception, are eternally secure in the love of God.[32] These are the definite number of those referred to in Scripture as "his own," "the elect," "the church." They are the ones Christ unfailingly gathers into his church and kingdom.

The denial of particularism amounts to a denial of sovereign grace, according to B. B. Warfield: "Particularism is the mark of Calvinism. The Calvinist is he who holds with full consciousness that God the Lord, in his saving operations, deals not generally with mankind at large, but particularly with the individuals who are actually saved."[33] This statement reflects the confession made in the Canons of Dort that the elect cannot be cast away, "nor their number diminished" (I, 11).

Although biblical universalism embraces the particularism of Scripture, namely, that Christ gave his life only for "his sheep," "his own," "the elect," "the church," or "those given him by the Father," it differs from the historic expressions of Calvinism in that it defines "his sheep," "his own" or "the elect," as being all

---

[31]*Redemption*, pp. 65-69.

[32]John H. Gerstner, "The Atonement and the Purpose of God," *Tenth: An Evangelical Quarterly* (July 1978), pp. 9, 10, demonstrates that in Rom. 8:29, 30 "foreknew" cannot mean "foreseeing their faith." The third step, "called," can be nothing other than the call to faith. Clearly the meaning cannot be: "Whom he foreknew as believing he predestined to call to belief." "Foreknew" has a second meaning as used here, "whom he foreknew as his own," or "whom he foreloved." See also Steele and Thomas, *Calvinism*, pp. 85-91.

[33]*The Plan of Salvation*, p. 87.

persons except those who the Bible declares will be lost.

The particularistic texts of Scripture and the universalistic texts have reference to the same individuals. Particularism in itself neither includes everyone nor excludes some. It addresses itself to the effectiveness of the atonement for all those who are "in Christ." Consequently the charge that particularism is "a radical misconception that leads to isolation"[34] cannot be sustained.

William Cunningham recognized the correlation between the universalistic and the particularistic texts, and he stressed that both types of texts have reference to the same people:

> It is the same love of God to men, the same death of Christ, and the same ransom price paid for men, that are connected both with the limited and unlimited phraseology. God *loved* the world, and Christ *loved* His church; Christ *died* for all, and He *died* for His sheep; He *gave Himself a ransom* for all, and He *gave Himself a ransom* for many; and there is no warrant whatever for alleging that, in the one case, the love and death and the ransom are descriptive of totally different things from what they describe in the other. The very same things are predicated of the two classes, the all and the sheep, the all and the many; and, *therefore,* the fair inference is, that *they are not really two different classes, but one and the same class,* somewhat differently described and, of course, regarded under somewhat different aspects.[35]

Cunningham then faults Arminianism because it does "not predicate the same but different things, of the two classes — the all and the sheep, the all and the many — while the Scripture predicates the same, and not different things of both."[36]

Particular atonement teaches that all those and only those for whom Christ died will be saved. The limited phraseology of the particularistic texts ("the many") and the unlimited phraseology of the universalistic texts ("all men"), with the exceptions imposed by the teachings of Scripture in general, have reference to the same individuals, that is, to those who are "in Christ." In each instance the immediate context dictated for the biblical writer the choice between the limited or unlimited phrasing of the

[34]Berkouwer, *Divine Election,* p. 315.

[35]*Historical Theology* (London: The Banner of Truth Trust, 1960), II, 343.

[36]*Ibid.*

reference. The limited phraseology and the unlimited phraseology referring to those for whom Christ died can be harmonized only by accepting the premise that all are elect in Christ except those who the Scripture declares will be lost.

Who ultimately decides whether someone will be saved or lost? This question has served as a familiar touchstone to determine whether one is a Calvinist (who believes in particular atonement) or an Arminian (who believes in a universal atonement). Presumably the Calvinist would not hesitate to say it is God who makes the determination, and the Arminian could not deny that it is a decision made by a person. In the light of what has been presented in this chapter we must say that this is no "either-or" situation. For those who are lost the blame lies in their own decision; Scripture reveals no other cause than their own sin and unbelief. For those who are saved, it is God alone who elects and saves them.

Biblical universalism underscores this truth, which echoes clearly in the heart of every believer: when one is lost, the fault is entirely his or her own; when one is saved, the glory is entirely God's.

CHAPTER VIII

God's Written Word
Addressed to All Persons

THE New Testament epistles are addressed either to churches or to individual Christians. They are written to "the saints" or "the brethren": those who are presumed to be in Christ. The readers are called to a new obedience which is based on and arises out of a new standing in Christ. Those addressed are required to live as "new creations."

John Murray uses the following illustration to explain how a person's new status imposes new demands: "To say to the slave who has not been emancipated, 'Do not behave as a slave' is to mock his enslavement. But to say the same to the slave who has been set free is the necessary appeal to put into effect the privileges and rights of his liberation."[1] It was fitting, indeed necessary, for the New Testament writers to appeal to their readers "to put into effect the privileges and rights" of their new standing in Christ. The recipients of the epistles were commanded to do many different things, and the appeal was made to them on the assumption that they were new creatures in Christ.

Consider how the following passages demonstrate that what the New Testament readers are required "to do" is directly related to what "they are": "So you also must consider yourselves dead to sin and alive to God in Christ Jesus" (*to do*), because "if we have died with Christ, we believe that we shall also live with him" (*they are*) (Rom. 6:8, 11). Believers must not live after the flesh but according to the Spirit (*to do*), because "you are not in the

---

[1]*Romans*, I, 227.

flesh, you are in the Spirit" (*they are*) (Rom. 8:9, 12, 13). "We beseech you on behalf of Christ, be reconciled to God" (*to do*) because "for our sake he made him to be sin who knew no sin, so that in him we might become the righteousness of God" (*they are*) (2 Cor. 5:20, 21). "Therefore, putting away falsehood, let every one speak the truth with his neighbor [*to do*], for we are members one of another [*they are*]" (Eph. 4:25). "Work out your own salvation with fear and trembling [*to do*]; for God is at work in you, both to will and to work for his good pleasure [*they are*]" (Phil. 2:12b, 13). "Put to death therefore what is earthly in you: immorality, impurity, passion . . ." (*to do*), "for you have died, and your life is hid with Christ in God" (*they are*) (Col. 3:3ff.). These are but a few examples. In a large percentage, if not the majority, of cases, the imperatives of Scripture have the existing reality on which they are based stated or implied in their immediate context.

Paul's letter to the Romans is structured according to the principle that what the readers are expected, required, invited, demanded, exhorted *to do* is based on what *they are* in Christ. In the well-known opening verse of chapter 12 Paul appeals to his readers "to present your bodies as a living sacrifice, holy and acceptable to God, which is your spiritual worship." He addresses them as "brethren" who share in the "mercies of God." Most Bible students recognize that the "therefore" in this verse is Paul's way of calling attention to the fact that the doctrines of justification, sanctification, and salvation set forth in Romans 1-11 form the basis for the practical exhortations found in chapters 12 through 16. In the first eleven chapters Paul has spoken of what God has done for the readers in Christ Jesus. They are no longer to consider themselves under law, but under grace. It is because *they are* under grace in Christ that they are exhorted *to do* what he is now going to set forth in the remainder of the letter.

Many Bible scholars have referred to this theme of the relationship between believers and what they are required to do as the relationship of the imperative (*to do*) to the indicative (*they are*). Richard E. Howard stresses this relationship: *"The imperative is based on the indicative. It is because of the fact of the indicative that Paul could command the imperative. It was because of what they were that Paul could point to what they must be and do.*"[2] As we look more closely at how the imperative is related to the indicative, it will be evident that the two cannot be separated from one another.

In Romans 6:12 the imperative "let not sin therefore reign in your mortal bodies" is explicitly based on the indicative of verse 14: "since you are not under law but under grace." Says Murray, "Let not sin reign — this is the imperative. And it flows from the indicative. It is only because sin does not reign that it can be said, 'Therefore let not sin reign'; . . . it is for that reason that the exhortation can have validity and appeal."[3] The demand not to let sin reign has validity and appeal *only* for *those who are considered to be* "not under law but under grace," on Murray's view.

Similarly, discussing the new obedience required of a child of God, Herman Ridderbos stresses that although this new obedience is the responsibility of a person, it does not simply arise out of an innate goodness aroused to activity by Christ's example. Finding its origin in Christ, this new life is realized in a person by the work of the Holy Spirit through regeneration. "What is meant is that the new life in its moral manifestation is at one time proclaimed and posited as the fruit of the redemptive work of God in Christ through the Holy Spirit — the indicative; elsewhere, however, it is put with no less force as a categorical demand — the imperative."[4]

In his illuminating discussion of this relationship, Ridderbos portrays a person's new standing in Christ (indicative) and what is consequently required of him or her (imperative) as two sides of the same coin, unable to exist separate from one another. But the relationship between these two sides is not one of parity. A certain priority is found in the indicative: "the imperative rests on the indicative and . . . this order is not reversible. . . . The imperative is grounded on the reality that has been given with the indicative, appeals to it, and is intended to bring it to full development."[5]

We can see how this principle that the imperative is

[2]*A Study in the Thought of Paul: Newness of Life* (Kansas City: Beacon Hill, 1975), p. 134.
[3]*Romans*, I, 227.
[4]*Paul*, p. 253.
[5]*Ibid.*, pp. 254f.

grounded on and appeals to the indicative comes to expression in Romans 6:11. Concerning this verse, Murray says, "What is commanded needs to be carefully noted. We are not commanded to become dead to sin and alive to God; these are presupposed. And it is not by reckoning these to be facts that they become facts. The force of the imperative is that we are to reckon with and appreciate the facts which already obtain by virtue of union with Christ."[6] Since the imperative is based on the indicative, this imperative is therefore reserved for those who "are presupposed" to be in union with Christ.

Again, regarding 2 Corinthians 5:20, Hodge's point is well taken:

> *Be ye reconciled unto God;* this does not mean "Reconcile yourselves unto God." [The Greek word for reconciled] is passive. *Be reconciled,* that is, embrace the offer of reconciliation. The reconciliation is effected by the death of Christ. God is now propitious. He can now be just, and yet justify the ungodly. All we have to do is not to refuse the offered love of God.[7]

The imperative "Be reconciled to God," found in verse 20, is based on the indicative of verse 21: "For our sake he made him to be sin who knew no sin, so that in him we might become the righteousness of God." Berkouwer speaks about reconciliation in a similar way:

> Exactly in the words "be ye reconciled to God" we see the exclusive grace which comes to us in Christ as reconciliation. According to the structure of this faith it is perfectly clear that it is not a human participation in reconciliation. Elsewhere we have dealt with the correlation between faith and justification, which does not refer to a reciprocal dependence but to a believing acceptance of justification. The same is true of reconciliation.[8]

If reconciliation, like justification, is a matter of a believing acceptance of something accomplished for us — or, as Hodge expressed it, to embrace believingly the reconciliation "effected by

[6]*Romans,* I, 225f.
[7]*Commentary on Second Corinthians* (New York: Robert Carter and Brothers, 1859), p. 147.
[8]*The Work of Christ,* tr. C. Lambregtse (Grand Rapids: Eerdmans, 1965), p. 292.

the death of Christ" — then the command to be reconciled can be made only on the assumption that those so addressed are joined to Christ in his death and resurrection.

That the demands of Scripture are based on the believer's new standing in Christ must also be seen in connection with the requirement of faith. Faith is an act of required obedience. "To believe is the same as to hear and to obey, even as disbelieving is not hearing and not obeying. The obedience of faith, then, is really just faith — the total response to the gospel," Berkouwer says.[9] Ridderbos concurs: "Faith and obedience belong together and can be employed as interchangeable ideas, as can unbelief and disobedience."[10]

On the one hand faith is a gift of God's grace, the fruit of the Spirit of Christ working within the believer (indicative); on the other hand it is something demanded and required as an act which persons must do (imperative). Ridderbos brings out this twofold aspect of faith:

> There can be no doubt whatever that faith, however much it bears the character of obedience and submission to the divine redemptive will [imperative], nevertheless does not rest on the assent of man himself (that is, man in sin and in the flesh), but on the renewing and re-creating power of divine grace [indicative]. Were it otherwise, then the gospel would be a new law, and the whole problem of the impotence of the law would recur.[11]

Even the invitation, demand, exhortation to believe does not appeal to "the assent of man (that is, man in sin and in the flesh)" in order for a person to receive "the renewing and re-creating power of divine grace." Rather, "obedience and submission to the divine will" (the imperative to believe) rests "on the renewing and re-creating power of divine grace" (indicative). "The imperative is grounded on the reality that has been given with the indicative, appeals to it, and is intended to bring it to full development."[12]

Ridderbos makes the extremely significant observation

---

[9]*Faith and Justification,* tr. L. B. Smedes (Grand Rapids: Eerdmans, 1963), p. 196.
[10]Ridderbos, *op. cit.,* p. 237.
[11]*Ibid.,* p. 234.
[12]*Ibid.,* p. 255.

that the imperative not only serves to bring to expression the new life denoted by the indicative: it is also a means of *testing* whether new life is in fact present.

> Thus, for example, in Colossians 3:1: "if you then were raised together with Christ, seek the things that are above." "If" in the first clause is certainly not merely hypothetical. It is a supposition from which the imperative goes out as an accepted fact. But at the same time it emphasizes that if what is demanded in the imperative does not take place, that which is supposed in the first clause would no longer be admissible. [13]

If this analysis of the relationship between the imperative of what is demanded and the indicative of the believer's new standing in Christ is correct in the way Hodge, Howard, Murray, Ridderbos, and others have presented it, we have some perplexing questions to face.

How far does the presumption of being "in Christ" extend? The New Testament letters were addressed to visible churches as they assembled in an actual historical setting. The human authors had no way of knowing who were the genuine Christians among the recipients. Were the calls for a new obedience, which we may refer to as "redemption ordinances," addressed to all members of the church? Were only those who had received baptism presumed to have a new standing in Christ, and not the others? Did the human authors rather vaguely address the call to new obedience to the church, trusting that the Holy Spirit would direct the redemption ordinances to those who actually had a new standing in Christ? Was it left to each individual to determine for himself or herself whether the demand of new obedience had "validity and appeal" (Murray's words) for him or her?

Of all the redemption ordinances which find their basis in and appeal to the new standing that the believer has in Christ, is there any which is not required and demanded of all people? Surely the words "Let not sin therefore reign in your mortal bodies, to make you obey their passions" (Rom. 6:12) represent God's will for all persons. Does not God require of all that they put away falsehood and speak the truth with their neighbor (Eph. 4:25)? Are not all obliged before God to present their bodies a liv-

[13]*Ibid.*, p. 256.

ing sacrifice, holy and acceptable to God as their spiritual worship (Rom. 12:1)? Surely the words "Children, obey your parents in the Lord, for this is right" (Eph. 6:1) do not imply that the Bible School teacher must divide the class into two groups, those from Christian homes and those from non-Christian homes, and explain to the former that the basis for this obedience is their new standing "in the Lord," and to the latter that they must obey because at the dawn of history God gave authority to parents.

"We are not told in the Sermon on the Mount, 'Live like this and you will become Christian'; rather we are told, 'Because you are Christian live like this,' " says D. Martyn Lloyd-Jones.[14] In stressing that the imperatives find their validity in the indicatives, he goes on: "To expect Christian conduct from a person who is not born again is heresy. The appeals of the gospel in terms of conduct and ethics and morality are always based on the assumption that the people to whom the injunctions are addressed are Christian."[15] The application of this principle is not limited to the Sermon on the Mount: "The appeals in terms of ethics in every Epistle are always addressed only to those who are believers, to those who are new men and women in Christ Jesus. This Sermon on the Mount is exactly the same."[16]

The fact that the biblical summons to new obedience is inseparably related to a person's new standing in Christ forces us to choose among three possibilities:

(1) There are a large number of demands, requirements, imperatives, perhaps a majority of those found in Scripture, which are imposed only on a limited number of individuals who are presumed to be new creations in Christ. These demands are not made on the rest of humanity.

(2) The same demands, requirements, imperatives rest on all persons, but the basis on which these exhortations claim their "validity and appeal" is entirely different for one group from what it is for the other. The new obedience of believers finds its basis in the indicative of their new standing in Christ; the same obedience

[14]D. Martyn Lloyd-Jones, *Studies in the Sermon on the Mount* (Grand Rapids: Eerdmans, 1959), I, 17.
[15]*Ibid.*, p. 23.
[16]*Ibid.*, p. 24.

is required of all others on the basis, for example, of their having been created in the image of God.

(3) The demands, requirements, imperatives of the new obedience are addressed to all persons and find their validity and appeal on the same basis.

Is there any scriptural warrant for making the distinctions that would be required by the first or second of these possibilities? If, however, it is assumed that all persons are in Christ (as biblical universalism holds), then all the imperatives of Scripture are addressed to all people on the same basis. At the same time, it should be emphasized (as we noted previously) that if what is demanded in the imperatives does not take place, the supposition that that particular person is in Christ (the supposed indicative) "would no longer be admissible" (Ridderbos's words).

There were those in the early church who were not authentic Christians. The recipients of the New Testament epistles were a mixed group of believers and non-believers, but none of them had a right to consider himself or herself exempt from the redemption ordinances. Those who wrote the epistles were aware that not only the readers (both Christians and non-Christians within the churches) were under obligation to keep these ordinances, but that all persons are under the same obligation. The New Testament writers make no distinction between what is required of believers and what is required of all others.

In a broader perspective, we accept the Scriptures as not "the word of men but . . . the word of God" (1 Thess. 2:13). The Bible is the written Word of God addressed to all. The gospel brought good news to the whole world. The epistles were written to young churches called to beam the light of this message into the darkness of a pagan world. Greek, as a universal language, was used as a vehicle to carry the Word of God to all people.

Although the Old Testament was entrusted to the Hebrews and the New Testament epistles were addressed to the church, in neither instance is it to be understood that the ultimate purpose of the message is limited, either to one nation or to the visible community of believers, the church. Note the following: "I will give you as a light to the nations, that my salvation may reach to the end of the earth" (Isa. 49:6; quoted in Acts 13:47).

Although the church is the "pillar and bulwark of the truth" so that it may be preserved from generation to generation, the "mystery of our religion" is to be "preached among the nations, believed on in the world" (1 Tim. 3:15, 16).

God's written Word is not only sent to all nations, but it is also to bear on the individual conscience of everyone who hears or reads it. "But now he commands all men everywhere to repent" (Acts 17:30). Grace was given to Paul to preach to the "Gentiles the unsearchable riches of Christ, and to make all men see what is the plan of the mystery hidden for ages in God who created all things" (Eph. 3:8, 9). Again Paul speaks of Christ who dwells in believers as the "hope of glory," the one whom "we proclaim, warning every man and teaching every man in all wisdom, that we may present every man mature in Christ" (Col. 1:28).

The great Dutch professor of missions J. H. Bavinck made this observation about the fact that although the Bible is formally addressed to the church its message is a message for all:

> The Bible is a missionary book. This means that in the Bible the Gentile peoples are addressed in a direct and straightforward way. This is the mystery of the Bible, its twofold character. It is a book for the Church, a book which can only be understood by the Church; and it is at the same time a book for the world, a book in which the world is called to believe in Jesus Christ. In the Bible God is wrestling with the world, persuading, reproving, admonishing, beseeching the various peoples of the world to accept the truth and to be reconciled to God. [17]

The Bible is the one inspired record which reveals the counsel of God concerning human redemption. There is solid theological ground for its being translated into hundreds of languages and dialects: as the Canons of Dort state clearly: "This promise, together with the command to repent and believe, ought to be declared and published to all nations, and to all persons promiscuously and without distinction" (II, 5). We may therefore introduce anyone and everyone to the Bible in this way: "It is addressed to you, whoever and wherever you are. It comes not because we earn it, or deserve it, or sometimes even want it. The

---

[17]J. H. Bavinck, *The Impact of Christianity on the Non-Christian World* (Grand Rapids: Eerdmans, 1948), pp. 139f.

Word comes because we need it. It addresses personally each of us."[18] The one true God who created all the inhabitants of the earth, the only Savior, declares, "Turn to me and be saved, all the ends of the earth! For I am God, and there is no other" (Isa. 45:22). Jesus said, "Go therefore and make disciples of all the nations" (Matt. 28:19).

The Bible declares what God has sovereignly done for us through grace in Christ Jesus, and all persons to whom the message comes are required to respond in faith, repentance, and obedience. No one is excused from any of these demands, all of which are based on the assumption that those so addressed are in union with Christ. This presupposition gives us the right to declare to all persons promiscuously the promise of the gospel and the command to repent and believe. Because there is only one written Word for all persons, we do not find a division within the Bible, with part of its message to be proclaimed to believers and an essentially different message reserved for those who are yet unbelievers. J. I. Packer observes:

> Evangelistic sermons are just Scriptural sermons, the sort of sermons that a man cannot help preaching if he is preaching the Bible biblically. Proper sermons seek to expound and apply what is in the Bible. But what is in the Bible is just the whole counsel of God for man's salvation; all Scripture bears witness, in one way or another, to Christ, and all biblical themes relate to Him. All proper sermons, therefore, will of necessity declare Christ in some fashion, and so be more or less directly evangelistic. Some sermons, of course, will aim more narrowly and exclusively at converting sinners than do others. But you cannot present the Lord Jesus Christ as the Bible presents Him, as God's answer to every problem in the sinner's relationship with Himself, and not be in effect evangelistic all the time.[19]

In the rest of this chapter we will examine some typical passages to show that the redemption ordinances as well as all other biblical imperatives are addressed to all persons. Our evidence will be taken from the immediate context of these impera-

---

[18]Lester DeKoster, *How to Read the Bible* (Grand Rapids: Baker, 1975), p. 9.
[19]J. I. Packer, *Evangelism and the Sovereignty of God* (Downers Grove, Ill.: Inter-Varsity, 1976), pp. 54f.

tives, demonstrating that they are addressed to all persons distributively. The response Scripture demands, of faith, repentance, and a life of obedience—together with the basis, ground, validity, and appeal of these imperatives—is the same for all persons.

The conclusion has sometimes been drawn rather quickly that the command to "consider yourselves dead to sin and alive to God in Christ Jesus" (Rom. 6:11) is required only of those who have been baptized, because the context speaks of baptism (vv. 3, 4). However, as Murray points out, to require people to "reckon [themselves] dead to sin" because they were baptized is to attribute to baptism a power and significance it does not have. This would be a "sacerdotalist view of the efficacy of baptism."[20] The appeal to their baptism is rather an appeal to their knowledge. Those who had been baptized and who were mature enough to hear this epistle read should know and understand the significance of their identity with Christ. The warrant for commanding them to "consider [themselves] dead to sin" is found in the indicative of verse 2: "we who died to sin." The imperative is based on and appeals to that indicative.

Who are those who have "died to sin" (vs. 2)? They are those in whom grace abounds (vs. 1), that is, those to whom grace comes through the obedience of Christ (Rom. 5:17-21). The biblical universalism of Romans 5:18 (see Chapter II above) provides the warrant for demanding of all persons that they "consider [themselves] dead to sin and alive to God in Christ Jesus." Essentially this imperative is nothing other than the demand to believe on the Lord Jesus Christ. This call to faith also has validity and appeal only on the assumption that those so called are in Christ. If, however, anyone refuses to consider himself or herself dead to sin and alive to God in Christ Jesus, refuses to believe on the Lord Jesus Christ, the assumption that he or she is "in Christ" is no longer admissible.

All persons are called to obedience in Christ, since "he is Lord of all" (Acts 10:36). And this call to obedience is based on the presumptive indicative that all persons are "under grace." The imperatives "Let not sin therefore reign in your mortal bodies" and "Yield yourselves to God as men who have been brought from death to life, and your members to God as instruments of righteousness" (Rom. 6:12, 13) are rightly demanded of everyone, and are based on the assumption that all persons are "not under law but under grace" (6:14).

We mentioned that the "therefore" of Romans 12:1 has a very broad perspective, referring to all the teachings of Romans 1-11 (see p. 75). The pivotal point of these first eleven chapters is found in the analogy between the first and the second Adam in Romans 5. The appeal of Romans 12:1 to "brethren" who share in "the mercies of God" is an appeal made to all those who are associated with Christ in Romans 5:18, that is, to "all men" in the biblical-universal sense of that expression. It is because "all men" have come to "acquittal and life" according to Romans 5:18 that the entire list of imperatives found in Romans 12 and following is required of all.

The assumption that all persons are "under grace" is underscored in Romans 13 and 14. It is true that for various reasons Paul, like some other New Testament authors, draws a distinction between himself and his fellow believers on the one side and the "ungodly" or the "men of the world" or "the world" or "this crooked generation" on the other. This ought not to seem strange, since the reality is that there are those who live outside the "one camp" in "no man's land" (see Chapter VII above). However, there are occasions when Paul feels perfectly free to identify himself with his readers regardless of who the readers might be (see Rom. 5:1-11; Rom. 12, 13).

The way Paul interchanges the "every person" of Romans 13:1 with "he," "you," "your," "one," "one another," "us," "we," "the man," "the weak man," "every one," "each of us," and "I" is not carelessness. Every reader, regardless of who he or she may be, has the right to assume that Paul identifies himself and the reader as standing in an identical relationship to God through Christ Jesus.

One might object that Paul addresses all the imperatives in Romans 12 and the following chapters to those whom he considers members of the body of Christ, who consequently have an obligation to live in fellowship with each other and to present

85

themselves as a living sacrifice to God. The observation is true as far as it goes, but the further question is, who are those who are presupposed to be joined to Christ and are consequently under obligation to live together as a fellowship of believers? The answer — all persons. No one has the right to live apart from Christ and in isolation from the fellowship of believers.

Note also that Paul commissioned Titus to declare that the message of Scripture has authority for all persons. "Declare these things; exhort and reprove with all authority. Let no one disregard you" (Titus 2:15). Titus is not to permit *anyone* to disregard him when he spoke with authority about the things the apostle has mentioned in the preceding 14 verses. No one has the right to disregard the demands of God's Word. "Older men," "older women," "young women," "younger men," and "slaves" — all must give heed to the things Titus would exhort. The reason, the presumed indicative, the "supposition from which the imperative goes out as an accepted fact" (Ridderbos), is that "the grace of God has appeared for the salvation of all men," as the "for" at the beginning of verse 11 indicates. The imperatives are valid and make an appeal to all persons (vv. 2-9, 15) because they rest on the indicative which is assumed to be true of all persons (vs. 11). It is the biblical universalism of Titus 2:11 (see pp. 49f.) and the other universalistic passages which gives us the right to press the demands of Christ's kingship on everyone.

Finally, we must consider the all-important imperative, "Be reconciled to God" (2 Cor. 5:20). We noted that Hodge, Berkouwer, Ridderbos, Murray, and others imply that this demand can only be made on the assumption that those so addressed are joined to Christ in his death and resurrection (see pp. 76f.). Reconciliation, like justification, is "a believing acceptance" of something already accomplished for us.

The question to be faced is this: Can reconciliation be commanded of all persons, or is it required only of those who have given some indication that they are "believers?" Paul says that grace was given him to preach "the unsearchable riches of Christ" to "all men" (Eph. 3:8, 9). Reconciliation is certainly among the "unsearchable riches of Christ"; in fact, it has been described as the heart of the gospel. The Bible is God's written Word addressed to all persons, and it is the message of reconciliation: Paul says that God had entrusted him with the message of reconciliation (2 Cor. 5:19).

On the one hand, therefore, reconciliation can be commanded only of those who are assumed to be in Christ. On the other hand, reconciliation, as a vital part of the unsearchable riches of Christ, is to be preached to all persons. The answer to this apparent dilemma is found in the truth of biblical universalism, which is established in the immediate context of the imperative: "We beseech you on behalf of Christ, be reconciled to God" (2 Cor. 5:20).

If 2 Corinthians 5:19 (see also our discussion of 2 Cor. 5:14, 15; pp. 40-44) gives evidence of the premise that all persons are elect in Christ except those the Bible declares will be lost, we need not hesitate to be ambassadors for Christ demanding of all persons everywhere that they "be reconciled to God." Philip Hughes adds a further response to those who would limit the imperative of 2 Corinthians 5:20 to believers only:

> The insertion in English versions of the pronoun "you," although it is not present in the Greek text, [implies] that Paul intended his appeal specifically for the members of the Corinthian church. In our judgment, however, this is a mistaken interpretation. At this point the apostle is concerned with the ministry of reconciliation for the world at large rather than with its application to the special circumstances of the church in Corinth. He is referring, not to the requirements of believers, but to the evangelistic duty of Christ's ambassadors to go into all the world and announce the good news of reconciliation to every creature, pleading with men to receive as their own what God has freely provided in His Son. His specific appeal to the Corinthian believers comes shortly, in the first verse of chapter 6, but not here. For the present the concise economy of the terms in which he effectively describes his universal missionary entreaty is best reproduced without resort to the introduction of inessential pronouns, as follows: "We beseech on behalf of Christ: Be reconciled to God!"[21]

In conclusion, we must say again that Scripture is God's written Word addressed to all people. The imperatives cannot be

[21]*Commentary on the Second Epistle to the Corinthians* (New International Commentary on the New Testament) (Grand Rapids: Eerdmans, 1962), p. 211.

divided into creation ordinances based on God's having created all persons and thus addressed to all, and redemption ordinances based on one's standing in Christ and thus addressed only to a limited number of people. The presupposition underlying God's message to all persons is this: The work of Christ, the Second Adam, has counteracted the work of the first Adam in every instance. The supposition from which all the redemption imperatives proceed as accepted fact is that "all the descendants of Adam . . . are saved," that is, that they are elect in Christ.

The new obedience of faith, repentance, and a life of joyful service is demanded of all people everywhere. To say anything less is to destroy the overall integrity and unity of God's message to all. Because Scripture is addressed to all, those who hear its message are obligated to respond to its commands and to find comfort in its promises. The presupposition of biblical universalism that all persons are elect in Christ except those who the Scripture declares will be lost provides the validity and appeal (the indicative basis) of these imperatives for every person. This is the presupposition from which the redemption imperatives proceed as a requirement for all. If what is demanded in these imperatives does not take place, then the "except" clause of our presupposition takes effect.

CHAPTER IX

What Faith Cannot Do

A s we saw in the preceding chapter, the Bible is God's written Word addressed to all persons. Among those who hear its message proclaimed are some who, sad to say, reject its truth. But for many the Word is the means by which the Lord Jesus Christ gathers, defends, and preserves them as members of his church. In the obedience of faith, and with the assurance instilled by that faith, believers become fellow-workers in God's kingdom, people through whom God does great things. "The righteous . . . live by faith" (Rom. 1:17). Faith has a continuous and pervasive influence in the lives of the children of God.

The importance of faith in the life of the Christian cannot be overemphasized. But at just this point we must discuss carefully a unique issue. Our specific concern in this chapter is to see what role if any faith has to play in our becoming recipients of God's mercy. Does the human act or attitude of faith have any function in establishing us in the state of grace?

One way to express the purpose of this chapter is to say that it intends to demonstrate that faith is "empty." Faith cannot initiate our union with God in Christ. Faith is neither the effectuating cause of salvation nor is it essential for the extension of God's grace to man. Faith is not a factor in our being established in a state of grace. This is the one thing faith cannot do. Even when viewed as a gift (Eph. 2:8), faith has no role to play in bringing about our acceptance with God.

But what about Paul's frequent insistence that we are "justified by faith?" It must be remembered that Paul uses "faith" because many considered themselves to be justified by living in obedience to the law. The *grace* of God for them consisted in this: God was so gracious as to give them his law, so that by keeping the law they could earn acceptance with him. Had Paul used the expression "we are justified by grace," his readers would associate that grace with their having received God's law. Paul's point, in the words of Romans 3:28, is that justification takes place "apart from works of law." Rather than being acquired by works, God's righteousness (justification) must be received by faith, which is a gift of prior grace. "That is why it depends on faith, in order that the promise may rest on grace . . ." (Rom. 4:16). There are only two ways in which one can be declared righteous: either by deeds done in perfect obedience to the law, or by being given righteousness by God in the act of his grace. By using the expression "justified by faith" Paul did not imply that some human act was essential to justification. "Justified by faith" conveys the thought that it is really grace that justifies us, as the apostle asserts in Romans 3:24: "they are justified by his grace as a gift."

Salvation owes its existence exclusively to the gracious, eternal, sovereign, electing love of God. Biblical Christianity recognizes that no human act is necessary to bring about the extension of God's grace to us. Ephesians 1:4 makes plain that it is only God's act of love in eternity which determines our salvation: "Even as he chose us in him before the foundation of the world, that we should be holy and blameless before him" (see also 2 Thess. 2:13; 2 Tim. 1:9).

There is, therefore, no causal connection between faith and salvation. "He who believes in him is not condemned; he who does not believe is condemned already, because he has not believed in the name of the only Son of God" (John 3:18). Significantly, this verse does not express a causal relationship between faith and salvation, but it does emphasize the causal connection between unbelief and condemnation. The Bible never presents the alternatives of faith and unbelief as coordinate options, one effectuating salvation and the other bringing damnation.

Although we could readily understand and intellectually accept a direct correlation between faith and salvation on the one hand, and unbelief and condemnation on the other, Scripture presents the truth of the matter as more complex than that. The Bible never asks for anything in order that we may attain salvation by meeting certain conditions or doing certain things. "For by grace you have been saved through faith; and this is not your own doing, it is the gift of God—not because of works, lest any man should boast," says Ephesians 2:8, 9. "Only through the most absurd obstinacy could one escape the fact that this text rejects quite finally even the most refined doctrine of conditional merit."[1]

In his classic work *The Bondage of the Will* Luther elaborates the position of the sixteenth-century Reformers. He portrays sinners as completely helpless in their sin and consequently dependent for their salvation on the free, unconditional, invincible grace of God. This grace not only justifies those who come to faith but it is also the cause and source of the new life of faith in all who are saved.

According to Luther, we are no more involved or active in our new creation than we were in our original creation as human beings. Having been created human, we are equipped to function and cooperate with the power of God in our life, whether that power "occurs outside His kingdom, by His general omnipotence, or within His kingdom, by the special power of his Spirit."[2] When one is a new creation in Christ one is equipped to function and cooperate with the power of God in one's new life, even though one did nothing to bring about his new creation: "He does not work in us without us, for He re-created and preserves us for this very purpose, that He might work in us and we might cooperate with Him. . . . But what is hereby attributed to 'free-will?' What, indeed, is left it but—nothing! In truth, nothing!"[3]

Human passivity in the new birth is taught in the Lutheran confessions:

> Holy Scriptures ascribe conversion, faith in Christ, regeneration, renewal, and everything that belongs to its real beginning and completion in no way to the human powers of the natural free will, be it entirely or one-half or the least and tiniest part, but altogether and alone to the divine operation and the Holy Spirit.[4]

[1]Berkouwer, *Faith and Justification,* p. 190.
[2]Martin Luther, *The Bondage of the Will,* tr. J. I. Packer and O. R. Johnston (London: James Clarke, 1957), p. 268.
[3]*Ibid.*
[4]*Formula of Concord,* Solid Declaration 2:25.

The thought that there remains in an unregenerate human being enough natural power to want to accept the gospel or to be able to cooperate in the work of regeneration and conversion is said to be an erroneous view "contrary to the Holy Scriptures of God, the Christian Augsburg Confession, its apology, the Smalcald Articles, the Large and Small Catechisms of Luther, and other writings of this eminent and enlightened theologian."[5]

True, according to classic Lutheranism, the person in sin remains a creature of option. To deny all decision-making ability is to deny that humanity after the fall retained the image of God. Thus Lutheranism holds that certain options are still available to the sinner. C. H. Little mentions that within the limits of bondage a person still has a measure of liberty.[6] There is a freedom of choice between things subject to reason. This may extend to civil righteousness and questions of morality decided by natural human judgment and often in line with selfish purposes. A person in sin may avoid murder, adultery, stealing, and thus be a loyal citizen, a helpful neighbor, a faithful marriage partner, and a loving parent. However, the ability to attain spiritual righteousness is the work of the Holy Spirit alone, and it flows forth from the electing love of God.

Calvin, too, was careful in formulating the correlation between faith and salvation. He speaks of the emptiness of faith: "God deigns to embrace the sinner with his pure and freely given goodness, finding nothing in him except his miserable condition to prompt Him to mercy, since he sees man utterly void and bare of good works; and so he seeks in himself the reason to benefit man."[7] Faith is like an empty vessel, for "unless we come empty, with the mouth of our soul open to seek Christ's grace, we are not capable of receiving Christ."[8] To enforce this thought Calvin says, "For as regards justification, faith is something *merely passive,* bringing nothing of ours to the recovering of God's favor but receiving from Christ that which we lack."[9]

Calvin uses other metaphors to dramatize the emptiness

[5]*Ibid.,* 45.
[6]*Lutheran Confessional Theology* (St. Louis: Concordia, 1943), pp. 97f.
[7]*Institutes,* III, xi, 16.
[8]*Ibid.,* III, xi, 7.
[9]*Ibid.,* III, xiii, 5; emphasis added.

of faith. For example: "Faith, even though of itself it is of no worth or price, can justify us by bringing Christ, just as a pot crammed with money makes a man rich."[10] He derides the pride of those "who claim even the slightest thing for their own merits because they wrongfully retain the credit for grace that passes through them, as if a wall should say that it gave birth to a sunbeam that it received through a window."[11] Calvin concludes his discussion by saying: "Let us hold it as a brief but general and sure rule that prepared to share the fruit of God's mercy is he who has emptied himself."[12]

The Reformed standards and subsequent Reformed theologians have also characterized faith as having *no value* in establishing and determining our eternal destiny. In the words of Article XXII of the Belgic Confession, "faith is an instrument that *keeps us in communion* with Him in all His benefits." The emptiness of this instrument is underscored by the further observation: "We do not mean that faith itself justifies us, for it is *only an instrument* with which we embrace Christ our righteousness" (emphasis added). The Heidelberg Catechism (Q. 61) speaks to this issue as well: "Why do you say that by faith alone you are right with God? It is not because of any value my faith has. . . ."

Herman Bavinck says that Scripture teaches that we are by nature unwilling and unable to accept the gospel, and that "subjective — as well as objective — salvation is God's work."[13] "The essential thing in faith as a gift of God," Berkouwer writes, "is that it is based on this truly monopleuristic [one-sided] act in the election of God. Faith in its 'instrumental' character knows only of this one and sufficient, this absolute and merciful, 'causality.' "[14] R. B. Kuiper stresses that before faith becomes a human act it is already a gift of God:

> Spurgeon was right when he said that, if there is to be in our celestial garment but one stitch of our own making, we are all of us lost. Or let us suppose that the work of salvation is a chain of

[10]*Ibid.*, III, xi, 7.
[11]*Ibid.*, III, xii, 8.
[12]*Ibid.*
[13]Herman Bavinck, *The Doctrine of God*, tr. W. Hendriksen (Grand Rapids: Eerdmans, 1951), p. 381.
[14]*Divine Election*, p. 179.

ten thousand links. A chain is as strong as its weakest link. If but one link of the ten thousand is of the sinner's making, he is hopelessly lost, then let us once and for all cease talking about God's part and man's part in salvation.[15]

Berkouwer feels that although the dialectical theologians have emphasized unduly the emptiness of faith, they were nevertheless honestly striving "to formulate the Reformation concept of faith as 'mere instrument' and thereby put the contrast between faith and human works on open display."[16] He also recognizes that in order to honor the sovereignty of grace the Reformers and confessions speak "of faith as instrument as well as the emptiness, the vacuity, the passivity of faith."[17]

According to Emil Brunner, faith is "the empty form, which in and for itself is nothing, except a vessel for its content. . . ."[18] "Everything human in faith is 'unworthy of belief' and . . . "if faith seeks to be more than a vacuum, it is unbelief,' " Karl Barth said.[19]

But having spoken of the emptiness of faith, we must also look at the other side of the picture. In confessing the sovereign grace of God as the only ground of our salvation, we may not disregard the pressing necessity of faith, which the Bible emphasizes. Berkouwer warns:

> Let it be written in capitals, put in italics, that salvation is God's salvation, coming to us in the miracle of redemption, God's salvation which has been devised by no human mind and has risen from no human heart. None of this changes a letter of the fact that this sovereign grace *must* be accepted in faith.[20]

Every orthodox theology confesses the uncompromising, urgent necessity of faith. "Only those shall infallibly be saved who believe in the Lord Jesus Christ. According to the divinely revealed plan, salvation is by faith alone," says Matthias Loy.[21]

---

[15]R. B. Kuiper, *The Bible Tells Us So* (London: Banner of Truth, 1968), p. 82.

[16]*Faith and Justification*, p. 174.

[17]*Ibid.*, p. 178.

[18]Quoted by Berkouwer, *ibid.*, p. 172.

[19]Quoted by Berkouwer, *ibid.*, p. 174.

[20]*Ibid.*, p. 185.

[21]Matthias Loy, "Is God's Election Arbitrary or In View of Faith?", in *Lutheran Confessional Theology in America 1840-1880*, ed. T. G. Tapper (New York: Oxford U.P., 1972), p. 219.

Henry Jacobs draws on the Lutheran confessions in saying that "if God were to save one without faith, He would act contrary to His own word, and would deny Himself, which is impossible."[22]

James I. Packer calls attention to the necessity of faith in these words: "Whatever we may believe about election, the fact remains that evangelism is necessary because no man can be saved without the gospel." From Romans 10:14 ("How are they to believe in him of whom they have never heard?") he concludes: "They must be told of Christ before they can trust Him, and they must trust Him before they can be saved by Him. Salvation depends on faith, and faith on knowing the gospel."[23]

Donald Bloesch criticizes Barth's view that faith is only a correspondence to God's act of salvation in Christ and requires no correlative act on man's part to make it effective: "In my view the objective work of salvation definitely has priority over faith. . . . Yet for the individual Christian, faith is just as decisive, since apart from personal faith salvation is forfeited." Again, "The work of Christ on the cross and personal faith are inseparably and organically related. No man can be in Christ but him who believes."[24]

According to Berkouwer, Karl Barth's view that all people are both elect and reprobate in Christ makes unbelief impossible and belief unnecessary. In his refutation of Barth's view of election he stresses constantly the urgency of faith and the dire consequences of unbelief. Because this is a biblical motif, Berkouwer's dogmatics devote entire sections to it.[25]

Within the space of a few pages Berkouwer makes the following statements concerning the urgency of faith: "Decisions must be made, decisions of frightening consequences. The Scripture rarely speaks of salvation without mentioning this urgency of belief. The same urgency is apparent in warnings to unbelievers." He emphasizes the value of faith by showing its power in the lives

---

[22]Henry Jacobs, *A Summary of Christian Faith* (Philadelphia: General Council Publication House, 1905), p. 205.

[23]*Evangelism and the Sovereignty of God*, p. 97.

[24]Donald G. Bloesch, *Jesus is the Victor* (Nashville: Abingdon, 1976), pp. 123f.

[25]*The Triumph of Grace in the Theology of Karl Barth*, tr. H. R. Boer (Grand Rapids: Eerdmans, 1956), pp. 268-81; cf. *Faith and Justification*, pp. 185-99.

of the heroes of faith mentioned in Hebrews 11. "Does not all this speak to us of the peculiar value of faith, indeed, of its decisiveness? Is there any fault to find with one who preaches and teaches this imperative with unusual stress?" The Scriptures "preach the necessity of faith, and do it with an urgency which is existential to the core. This is evident throughout them. They do not offer us a note of information; they come with an importunate message demanding the answer of faith." Berkouwer further says that there is an indissoluble relationship between faith and God's mercy. Elsewhere he says, "Whatever the judgment as to the dogmatic place of belief and unbelief, *we will in any case have to take as our point of departure the seriousness with which the New Testament takes the human response to the proclamation.*"[26]

The Heidelberg Catechism adds its witness to the importance and urgency of faith: "Are all men saved through Christ just as all were lost through Adam? No. Only those are saved who by true faith are grafted into Christ and accept all his blessings" (Q. 20).

What we have said thus far makes plain the tension between the concept of the emptiness of faith—a concept that honors the sovereign, free, eternal election of grace as the one source and the entire cause of salvation—and the urgent, indispensable, biblical requirement of faith. Berkouwer formulates the question of the relationship between the divine act of election and the biblical requirement of faith precisely: "What human decision can have *real significance,* it could be argued, *given the all-decisive divine act* of redemption?"[27] In the remainder of this chapter we will briefly review how various traditions have tried to maintain the "real significance" of the human decision without detracting from the decisive character of the "divine act of redemption." We will then offer a critique of all these efforts, and consider how biblical universalism responds to Berkouwer's question.

*   *   *   *   *

"Man's total inability to respond to God by his own power is the necessary backdrop for Lutheran doctrine. As long as man is

---

[26]*Triumph of Grace,* p. 270.
[27]*Faith and Justification,* p. 196; emphasis added.

regarded as contributing in any way to his salvation, he might be saved by grace, but not by grace *alone.*"[28] This theme — representing the influence of Augustine — is one of the hallmarks of Lutheranism, and distinguishes it from nearly every form of Arminianism. Salvation is by grace alone (*sola gratia*). At the same time Lutheranism holds to the doctrine of universal grace, the teaching that God in Christ has effectively redeemed all people, so that whatever Christ has done for any one sinner he has equally accomplished for all sinners without exception. This reconciling grace is resistible, and wilful resistance of it is the only cause of condemnation.

Lutheranism looks to its doctrine of the means of grace to resolve the relationship between God's sovereign act of redemption and the significant response of faith by the human person. "It is God's will to call men to eternal salvation, to draw them to himself, convert them, . . . through this means and in no other way — namely, through his holy Word (when one hears it preached or reads it) and the sacraments (when they are used according to his Word)."[29] Lutheranism asserts that while sinners are unable to respond to the Word in their own strength, the power of the Holy Spirit invariably accompanies the proclaimed Word. This power enables all who do not stubbornly resist it to accept the message, believe, and thus be saved.

Lutheranism with its doctrine of resistible grace has not claimed to teach an "all-decisive divine act of redemption." It does teach that the Holy Spirit prompts all who hear the Word to believe and enables them to do so.

Lutherans have been unable to agree as to whether this work of the Spirit is the outcome of an absolute predestination or involves some cooperation on man's part. The *Formula of Concord* denied both of these schools of thought; it stated that regeneration is exclusively the work of the Holy Spirit and the reason all who hear the Word are not saved is that some resist the power of the Holy Spirit which accompanies the Word.

Non-resistance, however, is a human act, not consistent with *sola gratia.* To account for it, some turned to the doctrine of

[28]David Scaer, *Getting into The Story of Concord,* p. 83.
[29]*Formula of Concord,* Solid Declaration 2:50.

foreknowledge, defining election as "the eternal decree . . . of God, according to which out of pure grace, He determined to save . . . each individual who He foresaw from eternity would, by His grace, be in Christ unto the end of his life."[30] But this concept of foreknowledge in turn made other explanations necessary. Because faith, which is the object of God's foreknowledge, cannot arise out of a sinful heart, the doctrine of "prevenient grace" was advanced. Prevenient grace is considered to be the internal call and illumination of the Holy Spirit in conjunction with the Word preached, so that everyone who hears the Word is unavoidably confronted with a choice. Likewise, all who receive the means of grace are thereby brought to the level of moral neutrality—from which position they must make a determination for or against God.

Other Lutherans deny such a prevenient grace. Pieper, for example, says that "when a man is inwardly or *subjectively* changed to such a degree as to be *able* to accept grace, he is no longer the old, natural man who regards the Gospel as foolishness, but a new man, completely transformed within, who has . . . learned to regard the Gospel as the wisdom of God."[31]

Let us look next at Arminianism. Although there are many variations of Arminianism, we can see its approach to the relationship between God's sovereignty and man's responsibility in salvation by recalling its basic teachings. The followers of Arminius, called Remonstrants, proposed the five doctrinal positions summarized above (pp. 66f.). By its teaching that Christ's death does no more than create the *possibility* of salvation for everyone and its view that election is prompted by one's own volition to believe, Arminianism certainly stresses the "real significance" of the human decision. It does so, however, by denying the "all-decisive divine act of redemption."

Wesleyan Arminianism (sometimes called Evangelical Arminianism) differs from the system of the Remonstrants in accepting as biblical the teaching that humans, as the result of the

[30]Jacobs, *Summary*, p. 554.

[31]F. Pieper, *Conversion and Election* (St. Louis: Concordia, 1913), p. 123. For a complete discussion of the doctrine of *intuitu fidei* see also the response in Leander Keyser, *Election and Conversion* (Burlington, Ia.: The German Literary Board, 1914).

fall, have lost all natural ability to cooperate with the grace of God. Christ's redemption has a universal influence, which removes the guilt of original sin and provides the seed of spiritual life for every human being. This "grace given" is sufficient to enable one to cooperate with the grace of God, but it is also resistible. The elect are all those who use the seed of grace aright. The "real significance" of the human decision is quite obvious in Wesleyan Arminianism; but the decisiveness of the salvation purchased by Christ is certainly compromised, and salvation is not a unilateral act.

The traditional Reformed (Calvinistic) view, with its stress on the sovereignty of God, clearly recognizes the all-decisive divine act of redemption. Its teaching is that in Christ God has elected some to salvation. These are the beneficiaries of God's eternal, incomprehensible, electing love. For these — and these only — Christ Jesus came into the world to be a substitute in receiving God's judgment against sin and in living the life of perfect obedience to the will of God (Chapter VII). The Holy Spirit infallibly works the miracle of new life in their hearts, thereby making them able and willing to respond in joyful obedience to God's will. The rest of humanity is passed by, and they suffer the just consequences of their sin.

In this view the necessity of a human response is based on God's requiring, demanding, exhorting, and desiring all persons to believe. Without faith it is impossible to please him. Only by the conscious act of faith can you have the assurance that Christ died for you and receive the strength to "overcome the world" (1 John 5:4). But the *real* significance of the human decision has remained somewhat unclear in Reformed theology. According to historic Calvinism, the act of faith does not place the believing sinner in a new relationship to Christ. Faith is the product, the fruit, of one's union with Christ. As a Reformed theologian Berkouwer has tried to develop a theology in which the human act of faith has real significance. Hence his question: "What human decision can have real significance, given the all-decisive divine act of redemption?"

Let us look closely at Berkouwer's answer to his own question, because it is one of few elaborate attempts to establish the real significance of the human decision within the framework of

Reformed theology. Remember that our original question is whether faith plays any role in establishing us in the state of grace.

Berkouwer envisions "a bond created by God to relate faith with His own mercy." Often he uses the term "correlation" to suggest the nature of this connection.

> The term is, naturally, open to abuse; it could be construed as a relation in which both sides are mutually dependent and reciprocally effective. This sense destroys everything true about the relationship between faith and justification. . . . Faith in the correlation bespeaks the working of the Holy Spirit in directing man to God's grace.[32]

In this correlation Berkouwer acknowledges both God's sovereignty in the work of redemption and the necessity of faith.

This "bond" or "correlation" between faith and salvation involves a unique and therefore ultimately mysterious relationship, according to Berkouwer. Nevertheless, certain things can be said about it. The existence of this bond or correlation accounts for the urgent, repeated call of the gospel; furthermore, this correlation between faith and mercy makes a person's salvation dependent on his or her positive response to the gospel. Therefore the Bible not only warns against the serious consequences of unbelief, it also places as great an emphasis—if not greater—on the urgency and necessity of believing.

To avoid misunderstanding, it must be said that although a human act is involved in Berkouwer's idea of correlation, he nowhere attributes merit to faith, nor does he even hint that there may be a relationship of cause between faith and salvation. "It is the way of faith which gives God the glory in the acknowledgement that salvation is *exclusively* His gift," he says.[33] In another place he explains that Scripture "establishes the necessity of faith, and that without giving us a shred of argument for ascribing merit to faith itself."[34]

Yet Berkouwer does speak of election *to* grace in Christ. Because this is an election *to* grace, it cannot exist apart from or independent of faith. Faith is "the working of the Holy Spirit

[32]*Faith and Justification*, p. 178.
[33]*Triumph of Grace*, p. 278.
[34]*Faith and Justification*, p. 195.

directing man *to* God's grace," and even though faith is described in terms of emptiness and passivity, "such concepts in no way deny the activity of faith, its grasp of its object, or its working itself out in love. Faith is still *a human act.*"[35]

Reformed theology has always considered faith to be both a gift of God and a human act of the believing sinner. However, when the Reformers spoke of the "emptiness" of faith they spoke of the absence of any role for faith in establishing our standing in grace. In this particular matter Berkouwer, with his concept of the bond or correlation between faith and mercy, holds that *human activity is involved,* though admittedly a human activity directed by the Holy Spirit.

"The miracle of grace occurs in the act or attitude of faith, the faith that is roused by the Holy Spirit," says Berkouwer. The correlation between faith and God's mercy "is firmly rooted in the concrete human existence; it is far from being sealed in the Godhead."[36] In Berkouwer's view election and grace become a reality only in the actual moment of exercised faith. He is thus very critical of Barth's making gospel proclamation an announcement about a given state of affairs.[37] The Scriptures in proclaiming the way of salvation

> preach the necessity of faith, and do it with an urgency which is existential to the core. This is evident throughout them. They do not offer us *a note of information;* they come with an importunate message demanding an answer of faith. The insoluble relation offers the only possibility of preaching the sovereignty of grace and the earnestness of the call to faith.[38]

In his insistence that the gospel is not an announcement to inform people of an objective state of affairs, Berkouwer claims, "It is so pointedly directed to the concrete existence of man that we may speak of an essential correlation between faith and salvation."[39]

We recognize that the purpose of Berkouwer's emphasis on the call to grace rather than the announcement of it is to refute Barth's claim that the announcement of grace can and must be

---

[35]*Ibid.*, p. 178; emphasis added.
[36]*Ibid.*, p. 179.
[37]*Triumph of Grace*, p. 275.
[38]*Faith and Justification*, p. 199; emphasis added.
[39]*Ibid.*, p. 34.

made to all because all (without exception) are both elect and reprobate in Christ. One can appreciate Berkouwer's insistence that the proclamation of the gospel is a meaningful, vital, and urgent event—designed to call persons to faith.

But in stressing the necessity and urgency of faith in his concern to refute Barth, and to establish a "real significance" for the human decision, it seems that Berkouwer has contaminated the Reformed concept of faith's function *in regard to the matter of obtaining salvation.* He inserts an active human element which is unacceptable. This is similar to such statements as "salvation depends on faith"[40] and "no man can be in Christ but him who believes."[41] Recall that Berkouwer maintains that faith, in its correlation to God's mercy, is a human act and that "the miracle of grace occurs in the act or attitude of faith." This correlation is an "insoluble" bond which relates faith with his own mercy. Berkouwer posits the human act or attitude of faith as *essential* for the miracle of grace to occur, that is, for the reception of God's mercy. As we saw above, he holds that this "insoluble relation offers the only possibility of preaching the sovereignty of grace and the earnestness of the call to faith."

True, no one can be assured of, enjoy, or "work out" his or her own salvation (Phil. 2:12) apart from the human act or attitude of faith. But this does not mean that the act or attitude of faith is *essential* if the miracle of grace is to occur. The Reformers, as we saw, taught that no human act or attitude can be involved in establishing us in the state of grace and accomplishing our union with Christ. In this specific matter they insist that faith is inactive, entirely negative, empty, or completely passive.

The difficulty with all the theological formulations we have discussed is that they assume that Scripture teaches that all persons are outside of Christ except those who the Bible declares will be saved. This leaves them with the task of determining, on the basis of Scripture, *how* sinners are to be re-established into a right relationship to God through Christ. Impressed with the nearly limitless, urgent demands to believe and accept the salvation offered, Arminians and some Lutherans conclude that even

---

[40]Packer, *Evangelism and the Sovereignty of God,* p. 97.
[41]Bloesch, *Jesus Is Victor,* p. 123.

God himself is unable to save those who do not of their own free will make the "significant decision" to believe! Some other Lutherans and Calvinists conclude, on the basis of Scripture's testimony concerning human helplessness in sin and the undeniable fact of God's sovereignty, that salvation is determined solely by the "all-decisive divine act of redemption."

As to Berkouwer, he is rightly concerned to protect Calvinism against a fatalistic, Muslim type of determinism:

> Such systems can only produce conclusions in which every human decision, whether for good or for evil, is swallowed up in the iron order of the causal structure. . . . There can be no certainty of salvation, or a really significant way to redemption. Salvation disappeared behind the clouds of a lofty causality. [42]

Berkouwer's concern to refute such notions is understandable. However, the tendency to equate Calvinism with a fatalistic determinism is largely due to the historic tradition of doing theology on the supposition that all persons are outside of Christ except. . . . This formula encourages speculation about an arbitrary, mechanistically causalistic, or even capricious divine selection. The premise which we have argued is established by the universalistic texts, that "all persons are elect in Christ except. . . ." This premise reveals God's gracious nature, with rejection being wholly attributable to the recalcitrant nature of the one who continues in sin.

Because Berkouwer begins with the assumption that all are "outside of Christ," he too finds it necessary to account for the occurrence of grace in the lives of some. To avoid determinism and to maintain the urgency of faith, he concludes that there must be a correlation or bond between faith and God's mercy.

But if one begins with the assumption of biblical universalism, it is apparent that the act or attitude of faith is not *essential* to establish a saving relationship with Christ. The classic question of "why some and not others?" becomes a matter of considering why some are *not elect.* Either we say that they are not elect because God "passed them by" or we cannot answer the question of their non-election because it is not answered in Scripture, as we suggested in Chapter VII.

[42]*Triumph of Grace,* pp. 281f.

103

Contrary to Berkouwer, the Reformers did not view the act or attitude of faith as indispensable for the occurrence of grace; they rather held that the miracle of grace must happen *before* faith can be exercised. Union with Christ the vine is essential to produce the fruit of faith, for apart from him we can literally do nothing (John 15:5).

That the miracle of grace is independent of all human activity is the witness of the Belgic Confession, Art. XVI: "elected in Christ Jesus our Lord, *without any* respect to their works." Likewise the Canons of Dort state that "this election was not founded upon foreseen faith and obedience of faith, or holiness, or *any other good quality or disposition in man,* as a prerequisite, cause or *condition* on which it depended" (I, 9). And the Westminster Confession of Faith asserts: "This effectual call is of God's free and special grace alone, not from anything at all foreseen in man, who is *altogether passive* therein . . ." (Chap. X, ii; emphasis added).

Faith does not bring about a new standing in our relationship to the sovereign, eternal, electing grace of God. Faith is a matter of resting in, clinging to, appropriating with a personal intensity the good news of God's Word regarding our new standing in Christ. This state of affairs was determined apart from any act or attitude of ours by one "who saved us and called us with a holy calling, not in virtue of our works but in virtue of his own purpose and the grace which he gave us in Christ Jesus ages ago" (2 Tim. 1:9).

There can be no *essential* human act or attitude in establishing us in the state of grace. Any act, even though directed by the Holy Spirit, insofar as it remains the sinner's act or attitude, is tainted with sin and imperfect as a "polluted garment" (Isa. 64:6). "Even *the very best* we do in this life is imperfect and stained with sin" (Heidelberg Catechism, Q. 62; emphasis added), and nothing imperfect and stained with sin can be *essential* to our union with Christ. As Spurgeon noted, not one stitch of our own making is found in our celestial garment.

If an *essential* human element were required, regardless of how minute it might be (even the human "act or attitude of faith"), it would mean that those who die in infancy, as well as those who are mentally incapable, would have to receive salvation in some way other than the way in which competent adults who hear the gospel receive it. This problem gave rise to the concept of a seed of faith (*habitus*) planted in some individuals. Besides being extra-biblical, such a concept would not satisfy Berkouwer's *essential* "act or attitude of faith." Scripture knows of only one election to salvation in Christ, a divine election — divine in its origin, divine in its execution, and divine in its fulfilment.

That salvation is exclusively God's work completed for us in Christ is the lesson of the analogy between Adam and Christ in Romans 5:12-21. Just as no individualized personal activity is required for Adam's sin to be imputed to those joined to him, so no individualized personal activity is necessary to impute Christ's righteousness (the miracle of grace) to those joined to him. The headship of Adam and of Christ bespeaks a real, not potential, "solidarity" with all those joined to them.

> The one ground upon which the imputation of the righteousness of Christ *becomes ours* is the union with Christ. In other words, the justified person is constituted righteous by the obedience of Christ because of the solidarity established between Christ and the justified person. The solidarity constitutes the bond by which the righteousness of Christ becomes that of the believer. Once the solidarity is posited *there is no other mediating factor that could be conceived as necessary* to the conjunction of the righteousness of Christ and the righteousness of the believer. . . . [The] *immediate imputation in the case of Adam's sin provides the parallel by which to illustrate the doctrine of justification* and is thus eminently germane to the governing thesis of the apostle in this part of the epistle.[43]

Because there is immediate imputation of Adam's sin and also of the righteousness of Christ, with no "mediating factor" involved in either case, the question posed by Berkouwer becomes all the more pertinent: "What human decision can have real significance, given the all-decisive act of redemption?" If by this question one means, "What human decision can be *instrumental* in determining one's eternal weal or woe?", the response of biblical universalism is that it is only the negative decision, the decision to disregard or disbelieve, which is pictured in the Bible as having

---

[43]John Murray, *The Imputation of Adam's Sin* (Grand Rapids: Eerdmans, 1959), p. 70; emphasis added.

a causal relationship to eternal woe. As the Canons of Dort say: "Whereas many who are called by the gospel do not repent nor believe in Christ, but perish in unbelief, . . . is *wholly to be imputed to themselves*" (I, 9; emphasis added).

Our conclusion is this: it is the decision of unbelief and disobedience which is the instrumental cause, or an essential element, in causing God's wrath to be *carried out* against all who refuse to walk in the way of faith, repentance, and obedience (Chapter IV). There is, however, no human act or attitude of faith which is *essential* for the miracle of grace to occur.

If we accept this position, we must still account for the fact that the Bible not only urgently warns against unbelief and disobedience, but that it also urgently demands faith, repentance, and obedience. Indeed, it was Berkouwer's correct understanding of the Bible's urgent call to faith that prompted him to view the miracle of grace as occurring only in the existential act or attitude of faith. Remember Berkouwer's starting-point: "Whatever the judgment as to the dogmatic place of belief and unbelief, *we will in any case have to take as our point of departure the seriousness with which the New Testament takes the human response to the proclamation.*"[44]

There is a subtle but nevertheless very real hazard in attempting to determine the *essential* correlation between faith and God's mercy by beginning with the Bible's urgent call to faith. We can illustrate this hazard by considering the relationship of faith to salvation as this correlation is expressed in the Heidelberg Catechism: "Are all men saved through Christ just as all were lost through Adam? No. Only those are saved who by true faith are grafted into Christ and accept all his blessings" (Q. 20).

It would lead to error to take this question and answer as the point of departure for determining the essential correlation between faith and salvation. One could easily conclude from it that true faith is *essential* for salvation (in fact, this is precisely how Arminius mistakenly appealed to this question and answer to confirm his views).[45] This "true faith" is defined in the preceding

---

[44]*Triumph of Grace*, p. 270.

[45]Of Q. 20 Arminius says: "From this sentence I infer that *God has not absolutely predestinated any men to salvation;* but that he has in his decree considered them as believers"; *The Writings of James Arminius*, tr. James Nichols

and following question and answer as the faith which comes only through the preaching of the gospel. If, therefore, this faith is *essential* to salvation, then no one dying in infancy can be saved.

The context of Question and Answer 20 reveals that the authors are referring to an essential requirement demanded of a certain category of people, namely, mature, mentally capable individuals who have heard the gospel. It would be a major mistake to use this passage to specify what is *essential* to salvation, when it has in view only a certain group or category of people of whom the response of faith is required.

Similarly it is a mistake to try to determine the *essential* correlation between faith and God's mercy by taking as one's point of departure *"the human response to the proclamation"* (Berkouwer as quoted earlier). Those who are urgently called and required to respond in faith to the proclamation of the gospel constitute a specific category of people — normally responsible individuals who hear the gospel. From the fact that the response of faith is required of these individuals we may not deduce an essential correlation between faith and the obtaining of God's mercy. To use that which is required of only a limited number of people in order to determine *the essence* of when and how the miracle of grace occurs is not warranted.

Berkouwer's advice "to take as our point of departure the seriousness with which the New Testament takes the human response to the proclamation" has been the approach of many others. Suggests one Lutheran writer:

> For a time let us try to forget what God may have done in eternity, and let us see what He has said and done in time through His gracious revelation. Thus we may be able to determine the ground of His discriminations between the finally saved and the finally lost. What does the Bible say? We might cite hundreds of proof-texts, but a few of the outstanding ones will suffice.[46]

The Lutheran confessions and various theologians in that tradition have taken as their "point of departure" the human re-

---

(Grand Rapids: Baker, 1956), p. 221. If God predestinated no one but "believers," none who die in infancy and no mentally incapable person is predestinated to salvation.

[46]Keyser, *op. cit.*, pp. 31f.

sponse which the New Testament requires. From this demand of faith they conclude that faith is not *antecedent* in time to election, nor does it *evolve from* election. It is rather "a part of the divine order of election," "a component part of election itself."[47] Such concepts appear to be very similar to Berkouwer's "bond or correlation" between faith and God's mercy, and they also account for the teaching that election does not take place except in the existential moment of belief.

Biblical universalism finds the urgency of the positive act of faith arising out of a truth of Scripture which Berkouwer notes in this way: "There is really no excuse for taking the edge off the seriousness of unbelief. The Scriptures, in their proclamation of salvation, allow us no other alternative than to see unbelief in its most disastrous proportions."[48] It is from this revealed truth that the urgency of faith arises.

In the very nature of the case, all the demands, exhortations, invitations, and urgent appeals to obey the redemption ordinances come only to mentally responsible persons who hear the gospel. For such individuals not to respond in repentance, faith, and joyful obedience is to *disbelieve* or *reject* the will of God as it has been made known to them. It is this act of rejection or indifference (which may be categorized as "negation") which becomes the ground and cause of their condemnation (Chapter IV). Thus the church must *announce* the *good news* to all persons, preaching "the necessity of faith, and [doing] it with an urgency which is existential to the core."[49]

Barth is not to be faulted for his description of the nature of the call to share in the victory of Christ when he says that we are called not to "resist the *monopleuric* [one-sided] decision of grace but to live gratefully in terms of it."[50] Barth errs in claiming that all persons *without exception* are elect in Christ. Nevertheless, he recognizes correctly that the gospel is the *announcement of* an objective state of affairs for the elect informing them of what God has done for them in Christ. Their response must be to repent,

[47]Pieper, *Conversion and Election*, pp. 15, 82.
[48]*Faith and Justification*, p. 199.
[49]*Ibid.*
[50]Berkouwer, *Triumph of Grace*, p. 118.

believe, and live gratefully in terms of the one-sided decision of grace.

The illustration of sunlight may be helpful at this point. The salvation of God in Christ, the light of the world, has broken forth on all persons (John 1:9), and proud indeed would be any person who claimed to have participated in the creation of that radiance. All persons enjoy its beneficence except those who stubbornly close their eyes to it and turn their faces from it. We see a parallel of the awesome "real significance" of the human decision when we compare the warning given by Paul that the passengers could not be saved "unless these men stay in the ship" (Acts 27:31), with the good news he had earlier announced to all of them, "There will be no loss of life among you" (vs. 22). There is a triumph of grace in Christ Jesus which is to be *announced to* all people, and all share in this victory *except those* who "by their wickedness suppress the truth" (Rom. 1:18, 28).

Faith is not a momentary exercise of the will which once for all translates us out of the kingdom of darkness into the kingdom of light. It is rather that victory in Christ in which those who have been redeemed by the blood of Christ live moment by moment, and by which they overcome the world, not doubting what God has revealed in the gospel. The mystery of faith is seen in that those who believe look away from themselves to what Christ has done for them.

In this sense — given our establishment in the state of grace — we can speak of the human attitude or act of faith as we put our faith into practice. God alone establishes us in grace, creating new life within us. With the knowledge of what God has done for us and trusting the revelation God has given us, we must live in newness of life in every respect. "Work out your own salvation with fear and trembling; for God is at work in you, both to will and to work for his good pleasure" (Phil. 2:12, 13).

We have stressed that no human activity is needed in *establishing* a person in the state of grace. But it must also be emphasized that it is impossible to enjoy the benefits of Christ's redemption while avoiding the costly obedience of faith. The grace of God necessarily produces the fruit of obedience, and this obedience has meant suffering to the point of death for many believers. Those unwilling to pay the price of obedience should hear the warning of the apostle James that whatever faith they claim to have without the works of obedience is not the kind of faith which saves them (James 2:14). Dietrich Bonhoeffer rightly warns the church of its deadly enemy "cheap grace," that is, grace separated from the practice of obedience. Indeed, there is such a thing as "the cost of discipleship."[51]

The thrust of this chapter has been that nothing human — including faith — can be an *essential* element in procuring God's mercy for sinners. This is the one thing that faith cannot do, and thus in regard to it the Reformers described faith as "empty" because man is "altogether passive therein." It is the completed activity and the perfect work of one man (not the activity of many persons) that "leads to acquittal and life for all men" (Rom. 5:18). All persons receive this "acquittal and life" except those, and those only, who disregard God's will for their lives, thereby bringing condemnation on themselves. Such a negation is the only human decision that has "real significance" in determining one's standing in relationship to God's mercy.

A large question remains. How is it possible that the affirming response of belief finds its origin, basis, and cause *exclusively* in the eternal electing love of God apart from any human act, and the negating response of unbelief finds its real significance in the here and now of man's decision without a causal reference to God? The answer eludes us, and believers gratefully recognize that the responsibility for resolving this problem has not been given to them. Here one merely traces the lines laid out in God's inspired Word.

---

[51]Dietrich Bonhoeffer, *The Cost of Discipleship* (New York: Macmillan, 1976), pp. 45ff.

CHAPTER X

The Church, a Covenant Community

*I*F we say, as biblical universalism does, that we should consider all persons to be elect in Christ unless or until there is evidence to the contrary, do we imply that all persons should be recognized as members of the church unless or until they have withdrawn from its fellowship? Does the premise of biblical universalism leave any distinction between those who are members of the church and those who are not?

In this discussion we shall use Louis Berkhof's definition of the church as "the whole body, throughout the world, of those who outwardly profess Christ and organize for purposes of worship, under the guidance of appointed officers."[1] This "whole body" is described by Albertus Pieters as the covenant community of people:

> Note that this is a visible community, i.e., a company of men, women and children in families, including believers and unbelievers alike, so long as they remain in the circle of the covenant. Faith is the center, but it is a center with a large circumference, and within that circumference there is room for many whose connection with God is outward only, as well as for those whose hearts take hold of the covenant God and the covenant promises with true faith. It is not a company of the elect, but a social group, recognizable as such by the world at large. It was and is an earthly group within which and through which God was working out and is still working out His plans for an eternal and heavenly salvation.[2]

[1]*Systematic Theology* (Grand Rapids: Eerdmans, 4th ed., 1949), p. 557.

[2]Albertus Pieters, *The Seed of Abraham* (Grand Rapids: Eerdmans, 1950), p. 21.

111

From what is revealed concerning the church in Scripture and what we observe of the church as it exists today, we cannot say that the church consists of those, and those only, who have been redeemed by the blood of Christ and participate in eternal life by God's grace. There are hypocrites, pretenders, who are members of the church. What then distinguishes a member of the church from the rest of humanity? We can determine the answer to this question by considering what it means to be a member of the covenant community of God's people.

A covenant, in the biblical sense of the word, is an oath-bound commitment or promise, usually accompanied with a sign. John Murray speaks of two essential elements of the covenant of grace. There is "grace bestowed" and a "promise given."[3] For the covenant of grace to be constituted, there must be not only an attitude or disposition of God's grace toward human persons, but also a promise, a vow, an oath-bound commitment which explicitly declares the attitude of grace. Without such a vow or promise there is no covenant of grace. Scripture, unlike modern legal codes, knows nothing of an unexpressed, non-verbal, or implied covenant. Covenant, in its biblical definition, involves an *expressed* promise. According to Murray, Paul's letter to the Romans uses the term covenant "in accordance with the biblical conception of covenant as oath-bound confirmation."[4]

Because there is no covenant apart from its being specifically expressed with an oath, Calvin is emphatic in denying that the covenant existed before it was established with Abraham and sealed with the sign of circumcision (see Gen. 17:11; Heb. 6:13).[5] Louis Berkhof reflects the thinking of later theologians: "The covenant relationship between God and man existed from the very beginning, and therefore long before the formal establishment of the covenant with Abraham."[6] From the idea that a covenant can exist apart from being specifically and formally established, some

---

[3]John Murray, *The Covenant of Grace* (London: Tyndale Press, 1954), p. 31.

[4]*Ibid.*, p. 28; cf. *Romans*, II, 100.

[5]See Calvin's commentaries on Gal. 3:17 and Hos. 6:7. The covenant with Noah (Gen. 6, 7) is a promise of temporal blessing for all creation and therefore distinct from the covenant of salvation.

[6]*Op. cit.*, pp. 263f.

knowledgeable Reformed theologians conclude that all people are, because of their relationship to Adam, covenant people, and that the God of the covenant now calls them back to himself in the proclamation of the gospel.[7]

An attitude of favor is revealed to Adam in Genesis 2 and to the woman and her seed in Genesis 3:15. All persons would be made enemies of Satan and therefore by implication friends of God. But contrary to what is frequently asserted we do *not* read about the establishment of a covenant in Genesis 2.[8] All persons are not covenant people by virtue of their relationship to Adam.

No one can deny the reality of God's attitude of favor to the human race, nor the many good and necessary implications that flow from this. But biblical usage prohibits designating this as "the covenant of God's favor."[9] As Murray has shown conclusively, a "bonded and oath-bound promise" is an *essential* element in the biblical concept of covenant.

The covenant was initiated with Abraham, who received the sign of circumcision; and it was continued with "his seed."[10] Its content, as stated in Genesis 17, is that God would be their God and they were to be his children. The Lord said to Abraham, "I will bless you . . . so that you will be a blessing . . . and by you all the families of the earth shall bless themselves" (Gen. 12:2, 3). Paul calls *this* the gospel: "And the scripture, foreseeing that God would justify the Gentiles by faith, preached *the gospel* beforehand to Abraham, saying 'In you shall all the nations be blessed.' So then, those who are men of faith are blessed with Abraham who had faith" (Gal. 3:8, 9). The unique place of Abraham in relationship to all those who are Christ's can be accounted for only by the fact that the covenant was initiated with him. God's promise of grace and the oath-bound commitment to the believer together with his descendants came initially to Abraham (Gal. 3:29).

[7]Alexander C. DeJong, " 'God Loves All Men' — Continuing the Discussion," *Reformed Journal*, XIII (May-June 1963), 17.
[8]S. G. De Graaf, *Promise and Deliverance*, tr. H. E. and E. W. Runner (St. Catharines, Ont.: Paideia, 1977), I, 36.
[9]*Ibid.*, p. 37.
[10]For an enlightening discussion of "his seed," see Pieters, *The Seed of Abraham.*

The development of this community of people can be traced through various stages: the time of the patriarchs, the nation of Israel, and finally the New Testament church. "And if you are Christ's, then you are Abraham's offspring, heirs according to the promise" (Gal. 3:29). Pieters mentions that before the time of Abraham there were

> individual believers, but there was no social group, lying in the midst of humanity like an island in the sea or an oasis in the desert, distinctly marked out from all others by the fact that God was their God and they were His people. This began with the covenant of Genesis 17, and has continued until this day. We now call that community the visible Christian church. [11]

Ever since the time of Abraham this externally observable community called God's covenant people has continued to exist in distinction from the rest of humanity. Because the New Testament believers are the continuation of the covenant community initiated with the rite of circumcision, Paul can write to them, "For we are the true circumcision, who worship God in spirit, and glory in Christ Jesus" (Phil. 3:3; see also Col. 2:11, 12).

Biblical universalism recognizes that there is a distinct, externally noted community of people to whom God has verbalized his attitude of blessing and confirmed his promise of grace by an oath accompanied with a sign. Because an oath-bound commitment or vow constitutes the essence of the covenant relationship, all members of this community of believers, together with their children, are covenant members. There can be no distinction between *true* covenant members (those in whom the miracle of grace has occurred or will occur) and those who are *external* members only. Murray observes:

> It is worthy of note that although Paul distinguishes between Israel and Israel, seed and seed, children and children (cf. Rom. 9:6-13), he does not make this discrimination in terms of "covenant" so as to distinguish between those who are in the covenant in a broader sense and those who are actually partakers of its grace. [12]

God has made a vow, and sealed it with the sign of the sacrament,

[11] *Ibid.*, p. 14.
[12] *Romans*, II, 100.

to all the members of this community, that he will be their God and they shall be his people, unless they refuse to live the covenant life of repentance, faith, and obedience. Should they disregard his covenant promise they will never enjoy its blessings (Jer. 18:9, 10), and they will bring on themselves a heavier judgment than if they had never been members of the covenant community, the visible church.

The fact that God has a covenant people (the visible church) does not mean that his attitude or disposition of grace toward them is different from his attitude towards the rest of the descendants of Adam and Eve. It *does* mean that members of the church are distinguished from the rest of humanity by God's pledge of mercy and grace to them and his gift of the sign and seal of his oath-bound promise. Jeremiah was permitted to reveal God's thoughts toward the covenant people: "For I know the plans I have for you, says the Lord, plans for welfare and not for evil, to give you a future and a hope" (Jer. 29:11). Isaiah was allowed to reveal the essence of the unsearchable riches of Christ to God's covenant people in ancient days: "Comfort, comfort my people, says your God. Speak tenderly to Jerusalem, and cry to her that her warfare is ended, that her iniquity is pardoned" (Isa. 40:1).

Paul understood the mystery that he could now share with the Gentiles, which had remained hidden in other generations: This mystery "was not made known to the sons of men in other generations as it now has been revealed to his holy apostles and prophets by the Spirit; that is, how the Gentiles are fellow heirs, members of the same body, and partakers of the promise in Christ Jesus through the gospel" (Eph. 3:5, 6).

The situation was not that God had an attitude of indifference or hostility toward all the Gentile nations before the mystery was revealed, and that at the time of Christ's sacrifice this attitude was suddenly and drastically changed. God's attitude or disposition of grace did not change, but until the appointed time in history the expression and verbalization of his forgiving grace was to be limited to the one people to whom he had chosen to make his grace known by way of an oath-bound promise. From eternity the Gentiles were "fellow heirs, members of the same body"; they did not at a particular point in history become fellow heirs. The difference was that they were "strangers to the covenants of promise, having no hope and without God in the world" (Eph. 2:12). After Christ's death that which had not been known became known and was to be proclaimed to all persons. The Gentiles are fellow heirs, members of the same body, and partakers of the grace of God in Christ.

What distinguishes a member of the church (the covenant community) from a non-member is *not* that the covenant member is the recipient of a special or qualitatively different grace. The covenant member differs in having the gracious disposition of God made known to him or her and the oath-bound promise of that grace sealed in the sacrament of baptism. Similarly, the obligation to new obedience, which rests on all those who have been baptized, is the *identical* demand made of all persons everywhere — that they repent, believe, and live in accordance with God's will. Anthony Hoekema's pertinent observation should be remembered by every Christian parent and teacher:

> Not only children whose parents are not Christians but also children born of Christian parents must personally repent and believe. Membership in the covenant of grace (which is the privilege of children of Christian homes) does not exclude but includes the need for total commitment to Christ. The teacher should make clear that it is only after such a commitment has been made that a person can fully enjoy the benefits of a Christian self-image. [13]

It should be observed that baptism, whether administered to believers or to their infant children, is not the impartation of a new promise to the recipient. "A sacrament is never without a preceding promise, but is joined to it as a sort of appendix, with the purpose of confirming and sealing the promise itself, and of making it more evident to us and in a sense ratifying it." Thus Calvin expresses the relationship between the promise and the sacrament. [14] Baptism is the sign and seal of God's promise that he "will be their God." It is also a constant, solemn, yet joyful summons for the recipients to recognize the obligation they have to live the covenant life of repentance, faith, and obedience. The

[13]*The Christian Looks at Himself* (Grand Rapids: Eerdmans, 1975), p. 111.

[14]*Institutes*, IV, xiv, 3.

116

identical promise is offered to all persons, and the same response of repentance, faith, and obedience is required of all.

Because the same demands are made of all (see Chapter VIII) and the promises extended to covenant members are also freely offered to the rest of humanity, differing views of the covenant have emerged. On the one hand are those who reason that, since the promise in the New Testament is offered to all, we now have a "universal covenant."[15] Others maintain that there is a covenant distinctiveness, reflecting a substantive difference between God's attitude of favor and grace toward covenant members and his relationship with the rest of the world. This poses a serious question concerning the unity of the gospel: "Is there one gospel, for all, or are there two, one for the children of Christians and one for the children of non-Christians?"[16]

Although the premise of biblical universalism implies that there is no difference between God's attitude of grace toward covenant members and others, this does not mean the covenant has lost its distinctiveness. The distinctiveness lies in the oath-bound commitment, the vow signed and sealed by the sacrament of baptism, given to all covenant members. Because the essence of the covenant involves God's oath-bound commitment, and not the content of the promise, there is one gospel, one message, to be urgently proclaimed to all.

To say it is true for all persons, not just covenant members, that God "will be their God" and that they must also repent, believe, and obey, is not to say there is no advantage or distinctive blessing which accrues to those who are members of the church, the covenant community. When Paul spoke of the sameness of God's way of dealing with all persons, reflecting that there is no substantive difference in his attitude toward them (see Rom. 1:5, 6, 14, 16, 28; 2:1, 4, 6-12, 25-29), he anticipated the inference that would be drawn; and he responded by asking and answering these pointed questions: "Then what advantage has the Jew? Or what is the value of circumcision? Much in every way. To begin with, the Jews are entrusted with the oracles of God" (Rom. 3:1,

---

[15]Richard R. De Ridder, *Discipling the Nations* (Grand Rapids: Baker, 1975), pp. 139ff.

[16]Donald Bridge and David Phypers, *The Water that Divides* (Downers Grove, Ill.: Inter-Varsity, 1977), p. 51.

2). We might paraphrase Paul in this way: "Then what advantage does a covenant member have (since God treats all persons alike)?" The answer is, "Much in every way." The covenant member, the baptized individual, has received the "oracles [supernatural message] of God." The message is pledged to the covenant member with an oath from God. The baptized individual, adult or infant, receives a pledge of being nurtured in the way of faith and obedience. The advantage of such Christian nurturing within the covenant community is beyond price. Its purpose is so that all the members of the church may "attain to the unity of the faith and of the knowledge of the Son of God, to mature manhood, to the measure of the stature of the fulness of Christ" (Eph. 4:13).

God shows his covenant faithfulness by giving his oath-bound promise to believers, to their children, and to all who are brought into the community of believers; and within this communion provision is made for their spiritual growth. Murray correctly insists that "the import of baptism must be the same for infants as for adults. It cannot have one meaning for infants and another for adults."[17] Whether for infant or adult, baptism is the seal of God's promise together with an opportunity for Christian nurture. The intimate relationship between promise and nurture is depicted by Leonard Verduin:

> It so happens that God has bound His promise to the fact that man is a creature of nurture. We know nothing of any promise made with disregard for the fact that man is such a creature of nurture. In fact, it verges on the irreverent to put in the mouth of God such a sentiment as "I will be your God—regardless of whether you walk before me in faith and obedience," or "I will be the God of your seed—quite apart from what you do in the matter of nurture."[18]

Whether baptized as adults or as infants, those who despise the promise of God or neglect the nurture made available to them will receive the greater condemnation.

Biblical universalism does not remove the lines of demarcation between those who are members of the church and those who are still "strangers to the covenants of [= characterized by]

---

[17]John Murray, *Christian Baptism* (Nutley, N.J.: Presbyterian and Reformed, 1962), p. 48.
[18]Verduin, *Somewhat Less Than God,* pp. 160f.

promise" (Eph. 2:12). But it does reflect the truth implied in Genesis 3:15 that the friendship of God was established with our first parents and their descendants—all of whom will enjoy his favor, except those who wilfully and ultimately disregard his will. On the other hand, the oath-bound commitment or promise (the covenant of grace) established with Abraham and his descendants continues. God graciously seals his promise with an oath and a sign given (through the church) to believers and their descendants and to all who come to know and believe his Word: "For the promise is to you and to your children and to all that are far off, every one whom the Lord our God calls to him" (Acts 2:39).

CHAPTER XI

Infant Salvation

BIBLICAL universalism provides a basis for believing that all who die in infancy as well as all who are mentally incapable are saved. In this chapter we shall use the expression "those who die in infancy" to include those who are mentally incapable throughout their lifetime and never attain to a status of personal accountability. The biblical foundation for our belief that all such individuals are saved is found in Chapters I-VII. The universalistic texts establish the premise that all persons are elect in Christ except those of whom we learn in the broader context of Scripture that they will not share in the benefits of Christ's redemption.

The Bible invariably describes those who will be eternally separated from the presence of God as those, and those only, who wilfully and ultimately refuse to have God in their knowledge. Either by indifference or disobedience they disregard the law or will of God as it has been revealed to them (Chapter IV). The judgment, "So they are without excuse; for although they knew God they did not honor him as God or give thanks to him, but they became futile in their thinking and their senseless minds were darkened," is not spoken against those who have never been able "by their wickedness to suppress the truth" (see Rom. 1:18, 20, 21).

If therefore the universalistic texts establish the premise of biblical universalism, it follows that all those who die in infancy are saved. As we saw in Chapter I, it is in this premise that Charles Hodge found the scriptural warrant for the salvation of all who die in infancy. He says we have no right to place any limits on the "all men" of Romans 5:18b except those given in Scripture. Scripture nowhere excludes any class of infants, either baptized or un-baptized, born in Christian or heathen lands, born of believing or unbelieving parents, from redemption in Christ.[1] Those who die in infancy do not reject the revelation God has given in nature, nor do they refuse to believe the revelation God has given in Christ. Therefore we have no more right to exclude them from the second "all men" of Romans 5:18 than from the first.

Not all of the grounds that have been set forth to support the teaching of infant salvation can stand the test of Scripture. One of these arguments is that of *innocency* (Pelagianism), which holds that children are incapable of moral decision and that con-sequently those who die in infancy cannot be penalized. This view not only conflicts with the scriptural truth that Adam's sin was im-puted to all his posterity, but it also postulates a salvation ob-tained apart from the shed blood of Jesus Christ. Another defi-cient argument might be called *sentimentalism:* the idea that if we who have been created in the image of God cannot bring our-selves to condemn an infant to eternal punishment, then we need not think that God could or would do so. The plausibility of this argument diminishes, however, when we realize it is equally appli-cable to adults who will not be saved. We could not find it in our-selves to consign anyone to everlasting punishment. Nevertheless Scripture teaches us that there will be those who endure eternal judgment. A third argument, that of absolute universalism, holds that all persons by virtue of their creation are children of God and therefore could never be the objects of his eternal wrath. But Scripture does not speak of God as the natural Father of humanity nor of all persons as the natural children of God. Scripture speaks of those who are saved as having been adopted by God through Jesus Christ. The premise of this view is in error, for we are not natural children by reason of our relationship to Adam (see p. 143).

There are those who oppose the teaching of universal in-fant salvation by pointing to the children of Korah, Dathan, and Abiram (Num. 16:27-33), or to the entire generation of Israel that died in the wilderness (Deut. 1:35), or to the family of Achan (Josh. 8:24-26). But the Bible does not tell us that these deaths

[1]*Systematic Theology*, I, 26.

were necessarily an expression of God's *eternal* wrath. Further-more, whatever is said concerning the judgment which came on these children, it may not be interpreted as a penalty for the trans-gression committed by their parents. Although the Bible declares that Adam represented the human race and that therefore all persons are guilty of the sin he committed, it forbids us to think that God would punish children for the sin committed by their parents. All of Ezekiel 18 is an emphatic denial of such a possibility. "The soul that sins shall die. The son shall not suffer for the iniquity of the father, nor the father suffer for the iniquity of the son" (Ezek. 18:20).

Simply because many invalid arguments have been used to establish the doctrine of infant salvation, we should not conclude that there is no basis for such a teaching in Scripture. R. A. Webb mentions a general belief in the salvation of all who die in infancy, which has been the common faith of many Christians, of various church creeds, and of nearly every theological tradition. He acknowledges that this testimony is not inerrant, but he observes that "the presumptions are certainly in favor of that doctrine which the people of God, living in the fellowship of Christ and his Spirit, have come to hold as the result of prayerful, studious, honest inquiry."[2] A. A. Hodge's study of the history of theology led him to conclude that "Calvinists agree with Arminians that all dying in infancy are redeemed and saved."[3]

Any doctrine of universal infant salvation must take into consideration certain biblical givens. The first truth that must be faced is that "through the disobedience of Adam original sin is extended to all mankind; which is a corruption of the whole nature and a hereditary disease, wherewith infants in their mother's womb are infected — and is so vile and abominable in the sight of God that it is sufficient to condemn all mankind" (Belgic Confession, Art. XV). The Psalmist recognized this: "Behold, I was brought forth in iniquity, and in sin did my mother conceive me" (Ps. 51:5). Paul reveals the cause of this sinful nature of infants in that "by one man's disobedience many were made sinners" (Rom.

---

[2]R. A. Webb, *The Theology of Infant Salvation* (Clarksville, Tenn.: Presbyterian Committee of Publications, 1907), p. 7.

[3]Archibald A. Hodge, *Outlines of Theology* (Grand Rapids: Eerdmans, 1957), p. 416.

5:19; see also Rom. 3:10; 5:12, 18; Eph. 2:3).

A second consideration for a valid concept of infant salvation is that the truth, righteousness, and justice of God are so inviolate that the sentence of eternal condemnation must be carried out unless something intervenes to remove both the guilt and the corruption of this original sin. The only remedy is the atonement suffered by Christ. The benefits of Christ's sacrifice must be applied to those who die in infancy if they are to be saved (Acts 4:12). To be saved, these infants must be joined to Christ. He alone can take away their sin and renew them in righteousness and thus make them qualified inhabitants of heaven.

The third consideration for a biblical doctrine of infant salvation is that the application of the redemption purchased by Christ must take place prior to their death. Any doctrine which teaches a period of probation for infants after death so that they may exercise their "sovereign" choice to accept the benefits of salvation not only engages in extra-biblical speculation, but also concedes that infants *as infants* cannot be saved. Webb is quite correct when he says that such an approach is

> tantamount to the doctrine that none but rational and self-determining adults can be saved. For the dead infant to be saved, it must grow to maturity in the disembodied world, and there, in the exercise of a *post mortem* adulthood, decide the issues of eternity for itself. It would then be saved, not as a *pre mortem* infant, but as a *post mortem* adult.[4]

Although no theological tradition excludes the possibility of infant salvation, few theologies can, in a manner consistent with their basic structure, present a doctrine of infant salvation which meets these three biblical requirements referred to above. Any theology established on the premise that all persons are outside of Christ except those who the Bible declares will be saved will find it difficult to construct a doctrine of salvation for those who die in infancy. Any theology which insists that the recipient of the grace of God in Christ must peform some conscious act of which only a responsible adult is capable will have to violate its basic structure in order to be able to account for the salvation of any who die in infancy.

[4]Webb, *op. cit.,* p. 213.

Any theology which insists that there is an *essential* human act, attitude, or condition of faith which must exist for the miracle of grace to occur, will necessarily have to make an exception to this principle for infants who die in their infancy. This holds true for all theologies which teach that each individual must make a sovereign decision for good: either by reason of inherent natural ability, through an infused grace given in the sacrament of baptism, or by means of a prevenient grace. God, in creating man with a free will, they say, placed a limit on himself so that *he* is *not able* to bring anyone to salvation without the sovereign consent of the individual involved. For God to impose his grace on anyone without consent is said to be an outrage against human nature as given in his creation. "God Almighty respects man's sovereignty, and will not transgress or abuse it. He will no more violate man's sovereignty at the point of commitment, as a believer, than He would at the point of conversion, as a sinner. Man must use his freedom to choose to be saved, and must make an equally free choice in surrendering his sovereignty."[5]

But this view completely overlooks the devastating effects of the fall into sin, through which the human race lost its sovereignty and became bondservants of sin (Jer. 13:23; John 15:5). It also disregards the fact that whatever man was in his original creation, in Christ the saved individual becomes "a new creation" (2 Cor. 5:17).

This *essential* human act was laid in place as the foundation-stone of Arminian theology by Arminius himself when he formulated his doctrine of predestination. According to this teaching God did not predestinate particular individuals to salvation; he sovereignly determined to save a certain type or class of individuals, namely, those who would believe in him.[6]

Wesley defines this essential human participation for the application of God's forgiving grace as the condition of faith. "How are we justified by faith? In what sense is this to be understood? I answer, faith is the condition, and the only condition of justification. It is *the condition:* none is justified but he that believes; without faith no man is justified. And it is the only condi-

---

[5]R. E. Howard, *A Study in the Thought of Paul*, p. 168.
[6]*The Writings of James Arminius*, I, 216.

tion: this alone is sufficient for justification."[7] This conditional theology is expressed by the followers of Arminius and Wesley in such commonly heard expressions as "universal atonement is not universal salvation"; "God has acted for all men; now every man must act for himself"; and "If ever man is saved he must open the door."

Such statements concerning "sovereign" human choice in the matter of procuring a standing in grace are erroneously deduced from the urgent appeal Scripture makes to all who hear its message. Scripture's insistence on a "decision for Christ" is directed only to mature, normally responsible persons to whom the Word is presented. This urgency does not arise from anything inherent in the decision which is *essential to salvation.* The urgency of an affirming "decision" for Christ arises from the fact — as was pointed out in Chapter IX — that normally responsible adults who hear the Word of God must repent, believe, and walk in obedience or they will be guilty of rejecting God's overtures of grace.

On the other hand, if one applies consistently the teaching that faith is the one act, attitude, or condition without which no person can be saved, the possibility of anyone's being saved in infancy is ruled out. Historically, Reformed theology has posited an unconditional election to salvation and a grace of God not dependent on human response to make it effective. It is only such an unconditional theology which can, in complete agreement with its principles, allow for the possibility of infant salvation. Warfield makes the following assertion concerning those who are saved as infants:

> Their destiny is determined irrespective of their choice, by an unconditional decree of God, suspended for its execution on no act of their own, and their salvation is wrought by an unconditional application of the grace of the Holy Spirit prior to and apart from any action of their own proper wills. . . . And if death in infancy does depend on God's providence, it is assuredly God in His providence who selects this vast multitude to be made participants of His unconditional salvation. This is but to say they are unconditionally predestinated to salvation from

---

[7]John Emory, ed., *The Works of the Rev. John Wesley, A.M.* (New York: Eaton and Mains, n.d.), I, 387.

the foundation of the world. If only a single infant dying in irresponsible infancy be saved, the whole Arminian principle is traversed. If all infants dying such are saved, not only the majority of the saved, but doubtless the majority of the human race hitherto, have entered into life by a non-Arminian pathway. [8]

But are not faith, repentance, and obedience required for salvation? They are indeed — for every responsible adult who hears the gospel. Their absence in adults who have heard the gospel constitutes a *rejection* of what God has made known. Their absence in those who die in infancy is not an act of rejection. Therefore such infants are saved without repentance or faith. R. A. Webb sheds light on this point this way:

> Regeneration takes place below consciousness; faith and repentance are those exercises which reveal this subconscious change. Justification and adoption are primarily *in foro dei* — in the pretemporal forum of God: faith and repentance reveal these cardinal blessings *in foro conscientiae* — in the court of conscience and experience. . . . Faith and repentance are but instrumentalities, by which this subjective work of grace is brought out in consciousness and life.
>
> Consequently, since an infant dies in the preconscious period of its life, these instrumentalities of faith and repentance have no office to perform, for the reason that there is no self-consciousness to be enlightened. [9]

Traditional Reformed theology allows for the possibility of infant salvation. Biblical universalism goes a step further. Its basic premise not only allows for the possibility of infant salvation, but teaches that all who die in infancy are saved.

The premise of biblical universalism does not imply that all infants without exception are elect in Christ. It does assure us, however, that those *who die in infancy* can never be numbered among those who have disregarded God's will for their lives. We may conclude, therefore, that the death of an infant is evidence of this child's election and salvation. Stated conversely, non-elect infants do not die in their infancy. They continue to live to the age of accountability, and if by their own choice they disregard God's

---

[8]Benjamin B. Warfield, *Two Studies in the History of Doctrine* (New York: The Christian Literature Company, 1897), p. 230.
[9]*Op. cit.*, p. 281.

will, they bring condemnation on themselves (Chapter IV).

Scripture teaches us that among the assembly of the redeemed in heaven there will be

> the countless multitude of infants and mental unfortunates, who went out of the earth through the gates of death prior to their moral competency, lifting up their joyous doxologies for the Electing Love of the Father, which gave *them* the right to heaven; for the Atoning Death of Christ, which cleansed *their* lives from the guilt of sin; and for the Sanctifying Grace of the Holy Spirit, which made *them* meet for the saints' inheritance in light. [10]

[10]*Ibid.*, p. 330.

CHAPTER XII

Exploring Further

W_E have been suggesting the possibility of approaching Scripture and doing theology with a revised premise. The working principle that all persons are elect in Christ except those the Bible declares will be lost results in new ways of looking at many areas of concern; and once this new premise is adopted, these ramifications begin to emerge. We can do no more in this chapter than bring to light some of the implications of biblical universalism, hoping that this discussion will induce others to pursue these and other questions more intensively. Our focus will be on four topics: the cultural mandate, the question of "love or wrath," assurance of salvation, and motives for evangelism.

A. The Cultural Mandate

Biblical universalism has a bearing on how we view the injunction to subdue the earth (Gen. 1:28). God gave this command, often called "the cultural mandate," before the fall into sin. Humanity, created in the image of God, had dominion over every living thing (Gen. 1:26). But the response Adam and Eve made to this charge was totally unsatisfactory. Despite the fall, however, the cultural mandate continues to be the responsibility of all persons, including those who do not recognize or acknowledge their God-given task. The command to subdue the earth and to "have dominion over every living thing that moves on the earth" has been given to all humankind.

Furthermore, this mandate is to be completed in the Second Adam together with those who are joined to him as the new humanity. Although all things have been put under human control, "as it is, we do not yet see everything in subjection to him. But we see Jesus, who for a little while was made lower than the angels, crowned with glory and honor because of the suffering of death, so that by the grace of God he might taste death for every one" (Heb. 2:8b, 9). It is through Christ—through him who is "the image of the invisible God, the first-born of all creation"—that God determined "to reconcile to himself *all things, whether on earth or in heaven,* making peace by the blood of his cross" (Col. 1:15, 20). Only in Christ can we attempt to fulfil the cultural requirement placed on us.

Although all persons are under obligation to discharge the cultural mandate, it is only believing Christians who recognize that they are allied in a great partnership as they endeavor to exercise mastery over the world, even the universe. Indeed, as Lewis Smedes says in discussing Paul's use of the phrase "in Christ" in connection with 2 Corinthians 5:17, reconciliation is such that, planted firmly in the death and resurrection of Christ, it "brings a world of people back into partnership with God from whom they had been alienated."[1] Smedes speaks to the matter of *how* this world of people is joined in Christ. Our concern is to face the question of *whom* this world of people includes. And as we have repeated often, biblical universalism delineates those who are engaged in partnership with God as *all persons, except those who wilfully and ultimately refuse to live in obedience to the will of God.*

Just because there are so many who oppose the truth of God in Christ and who fail to follow him who is the source of all wisdom, the universal applicability of the cultural mandate is not diminished. The cultural task remains the responsibility of all humanity. It is a universal directive—even though not universally acknowledged. God's people, entrusted "with the oracles of God," must declare that "all the treasures of wisdom and knowledge" (Col. 2:3) are in Christ and that only in his light do we see light (Ps. 36:9). Therefore, in responding to the mandate given to Adam, we must not think of ourselves as engaged in a narrow, parochial undertaking. We are joined in a work to which the Lord

[1]*All Things Made New* (Grand Rapids: Eerdmans, 1970), p. 104.

of the whole earth summons all people. Christians ought not to isolate themselves from others as they try to understand, formulate, and seek to respond to their cultural assignment.

Only those who are in Christ can self-consciously do what the cultural mandate requires because, not only for the church, but in every sphere of human endeavor, there is "no other foundation" that "anyone [can] lay than that which is laid, which is Jesus Christ" (1 Cor. 3:11). So, Paul continues, "Let no one deceive himself. If any one among you thinks that he is wise in this age, let him become a fool that he may become wise. For the wisdom of this world is folly with God. For it is written, 'He catches the wise in their craftiness,' and again, 'The Lord knows that the thoughts of the wise are futile' " (1 Cor. 3:18-20). The first six verses of Proverbs imply that the broad compass of wisdom, instruction, understanding, and learning have as their first principle "The fear of the Lord is the beginning of knowledge" (Prov. 1:7).

In working culturally Christians should not create the impression that there are many "foundations" on which one can build in fulfilling God's mandate. Taught by Christ and filled with his Spirit, Christians are meek, gentle, and kindly in their associations with their fellow humans. But they must be strong and unyielding in insisting that all persons must give allegiance to Christ as their Savior, Lord, and King. In every sphere they are to take "every thought captive to obey Christ" (2 Cor. 10:5).

Believers must regard all others as joined with them in obeying the cultural mandate unless and until those with whom they work reject the revelation God has given in nature and dissociate themselves from the knowledge and truth of God in Christ. Christians have a responsibility to challenge others to discover, rejoice in, and be obedient to God's laws as these are made known in nature, as seen through what have sometimes been called the eyeglasses of Scripture. It is the duty of all persons to live in obedience to the imperatives of Scripture both in terms of their personal standing before God and in terms of the cultural mandate.

Biblical universalism necessarily implies that we may never propagate or cultivate the point of separation between belief and unbelief (the antithesis) simply to make that division become apparent to everyone. God's Word is not intended to engender opposition or to arouse hostility. To be sure, the antithesis does come to expression. There is a distinction between those who serve the Lord and those who do not (Mal. 3:18). This is to be recognized as a reality arising out of the darkness of sin and the persistence of unbelief. Opposition to both truth and righteousness emerges in every field of knowledge and in every cultural endeavor. This opposition is a by-product of sin and a source of grief for all who desire that every person should live in obedience to the will of God.

The task of the church, therefore, is to call everyone to live obediently in and through Jesus Christ. The response required of all persons includes not only repentance and faith but also obedience to everything the Lord has commanded. An obedient Christianity will make itself felt in all areas of life. It will press the claims of Christ's kingship in the social order. Emil Brunner says of culture that "the Christian 'enters' into this sphere in order that he may impregnate it . . . with the ethos of the obedience of faith, and also that from the standpoint of faith he may understand it in its (relative) autonomy, and determine its limits."[2]

The demand made of all persons to be joined in the task assigned the new humanity of fulfilling the cultural mandate "in Christ" is possible only on the assumption that all persons are in Christ. Then if what is demanded in the imperative does not take place, the supposed indicative ("they are in Christ") is no longer admissible (see pp. 78f.). Without obedient faith in every dimension of life it is impossible to please God. God in Christ gives a gracious victory to all persons — except those who wilfully refuse to be joined with the new humanity in gratefully fulfilling the cultural mandate. By this, their disobedience, they exclude themselves from the blessing of God in Christ Jesus our Lord.

B. A Message of Love or Wrath?

The purpose in bringing the gospel is that those who hear may repent and believe. Jesus himself showed the way: "[He] came into Galilee, preaching the gospel of God, and saying, 'The time is fulfilled, and the kingdom of God is at hand; repent, and believe in

[2]Emil Brunner, *The Divine Imperative,* tr. O. Wyon (Philadelphia: Westminster, 1947), p. 484.

the gospel' " (Mark 1:14, 15). Later, after his ascension, came the apostles, "testifying both to Jews and to Greeks of repentance to God and of faith in our Lord Jesus Christ" (Acts 20:21). In Chapter IX we discussed the urgency of faith. The urgency of re-pentance — as a parallel truth — is also stressed in Scripture (see Matt. 3:2; 4:17; Mark 6:12; Luke 5:32; 13:3; Acts 3:19; 17:30; 26:20).

There is a valid scriptural reason for announcing the divine anger against sin and the threat of judgment in order that sinners may recognize the need to repent and to turn to Christ as their only refuge. At times, the most effective method of persuad-ing people to repent and believe is to tell them of the desperate and dangerous situation in which they place themselves by their obstinacy.

Nevertheless, we must not assume that it is first of all nec-essary to warn sinners of impending disaster, to tell them that be-cause God is displeased with their sin they are living on the brink of hell. Faithfulness in evangelism requires that we understand that it is not only the truth of God's anger but also the revelation of his kindness that can lead to repentance and faith (Rom. 2:4). All persons are elect in Christ except those who refuse to have God in their knowledge — this is the good news Scripture declares in the universalistic texts. The Holy Spirit uses the revelation of the goodness of God in Christ to lead sinners to repentance and faith. The positive and unqualified proclamation of God's forgiving grace is an effective means of arousing interest in the hearts of those who feel rejected by God or their fellow human beings. The premise of biblical universalism furnishes biblical warrant for bringing the good news to the whole world.

Biblical universalism impels us to declare to others the grace which comes to them — and to us — in Jesus Christ. The as-sumption with which we work is that all persons are elect in Christ. On the basis of this assumption we must tell all people what God has done for them in his Son! The awesome truth about God's wrath is to be reserved for those who remain indifferent to or reject this good news which the church has been commissioned to proclaim to *all people*.

There is an evident correlation between penitence and divine grace: the two cannot exist separately. But they are not mutually dependent. Grace has a priority! We need not wait until we see evidence of penitence before we proclaim the good news of forgiveness. "God's kindness is meant to lead you to repentance" (Rom. 2:4). Penitence (godly sorrow for sin), like faith, is a gift of God (Acts 5:31; 11:18; 2 Tim. 2:25), finding its origin in the fact that the penitent sinner is one who is joined to Christ and is the recipient of God's grace. The recipient of God's "kindness" is moved to repentance by that kindness. For "while we were enemies we were reconciled to God by the death of his Son" (Rom. 5:10).

It is not the purpose of the gospel to explain the terms by which sinners can induce God to grant them remission of sins. The gospel proclaims that God has freely forgiven sins for Christ's sake. He has taken their place on death row. Sinners must repent and accept this testimony of God's Word in faith and by obedience. To consider repentance as anything other than a gift of God, the fruit of the regenerating work of the Holy Spirit, is to direct sinners to look to themselves and to find their acceptance with God through something they have done or must do—namely, repent of their sin.

Repentance is no more a cause or condition of one's being joined in life-giving union with Jesus Christ than are faith and obedience. Repentance is the fruit of the Spirit of Christ working in our lives. All mentally responsible persons who have God's Word proclaimed to them must repent, and without repentance they will not be saved.

But we must press the question why we cannot be saved without repentance. Is it because God has established an *essential* bond or correlation between repentance and the miracle of grace, so that only those who repent can be saved? No. Is it because God has elected those and those only who would repent? No. Infants and mentally incapable individuals cannot repent, but they are not on that account excluded from salvation. The situation is this: those mentally responsible individuals to whom God addresses the gospel message who do not repent, believe, and obey thus reject the testimony of God's Word. They bring condemnation on themselves. Because they rebel against the revealed will of God, they must be told that the wrath of God rests on them.

Christ was sent to "proclaim release to the captives" (Luke 4:18). As Paul told the Ephesians, "he came and preached peace to you who were far off and peace to those who were near" (Eph. 2:17). The absence of peace and the resulting sword of which Jesus had spoken (Matt. 10:34) was not an allusion to a division between God and those to whom the good news would come, but a reference to the hostility which would ensue between those who accept and those who reject the message of peace. In other words, it is a reference to the antithesis. The message itself, however, consists in the publication of peace between God and man.

We may expect a favorable response when our primary message in evangelism is the unconditional release of those who are in bondage to sin. The proclamation of peace to men and women is possible because Christ has reconciled us to God and brought hostility to an end (Eph. 2:16). To say that our first purpose in bringing the Word is to make the hearers tremble before the wrath of God is sub-Christian. God's grace is the loud accent of the message of Scripture, and God's wrath is threatened so men may accept his overture of grace.

There are many searching souls whose thoughts "accuse them" and whose "conscience also bears witness" against them (Rom. 2:15). They are deeply troubled because they know they have provoked the just anger of an invisible and awesome power. The extremes to which many go in sacrificing their possessions, their bodies, and even their own children, in order to appease the "gods" whom they imagine as being against them testifies to the seriousness with which they view their own plight. Although civilized people express these fears and anxieties in different, subtle, and often unrecognized ways, they demonstrate that the requirements of God's law written on their hearts accuse them. "O that we might see some good!" (Ps. 4:6) is the plaintive cry of all except those who have stubbornly hardened themselves in sin. Henry David Thoreau was right: "The mass of men live lives of quiet desperation."

Why desperation? God's general revelation informs them that they are without excuse! J. H. Bavinck points up this truth when he says that all those to whom the gospel comes have previously heard God speak. The message of the gospel is *never* the opening statement between a person and God. God has already revealed his eternal power and Godhead to each person and has written the requirements of his law in his or her heart. Each one is without excuse. Says Bavinck, "Yes, the preacher of the gospel has a starting-point. He does not open the dialogue between God and his listeners; he merely opens a new chapter."[3] The new chapter revealed in the gospel is the message of God's forgiving grace in Christ Jesus. The one thing they do not know, apart from the gospel, is that the same holiness which accuses them has provided propitiation for their sins. Therefore they need no longer appease God's wrath or try to merit divine favor by what they do.

It is an error to think there is anything that must be done to inherit eternal life. When we bring the message of Scripture, we must be careful not to create the impression that human repentance, faith, and obedience contribute in even the smallest way to divine forgiveness. What must be proclaimed is the free, unconditional, sovereign forgiveness of sins, resting not on penitence, not on faith, not on good works of any kind—a forgiveness which is free because we are in Jesus Christ (Rom. 5:18b). Whoever brings the Word of God must *assume* that those who are being addressed are "elect in Christ." All hearers must be challenged to beware of bringing judgment upon themselves by rejecting God's gracious offer of salvation. Sinners must be urged to behold the mercy of God and so "consider [themselves] dead to sin," and to present their bodies "as a living sacrifice, holy and acceptable to God, which is your spiritual worship" (Rom. 6:11; 12:1).

Messengers of the good news must identify themselves with those to whom they bring their message. They must say with Paul: "In Christ God was reconciling the world to himself, not counting their trespasses against them, and entrusting to us the message of reconciliation. So we are ambassadors for Christ, God making his appeal through us. We beseech you on behalf of Christ, be reconciled to God. For our sake he made him to be sin who knew no sin, so that in him we might become the righteousness of God" (2 Cor. 5:19-21). When sinners remain indifferent to this good news or harden themselves against it, God remains gracious as he, through his ambassadors, warns them to flee his wrath which is sure to come.

[3]J. H. Bavinck, *The Impact of Christianity on the Non-Christian World* (Grand Rapids: Eerdmans, 1948), p. 110.

C. Assurance of Salvation

We experience assurance of personal salvation only when we realize that salvation is completely a work of God. To insert any human act or attitude as an *essential* element in establishing one in the state of grace is to subject the believer to perpetual uncertainty. J. Gresham Machen brings this to light:

> Acceptance with God is not something we earn; it is not something that is subject to the wretched uncertainties of human endeavor; it is the free gift of God. It may seem strange that we should be received by the holy God as His children; but God has chosen to receive us; it has been done on His responsibility not ours; He has a right to receive whom He will into His presence; and in the mystery of His grace He has chosen to receive us.[4]

The security we have is that we are in Christ. This union with Christ is not our achievement. We are not saved by anything we do—not even by our "decision" to believe. The "decision" to believe is evidence of our salvation; it is not a condition for being accepted by God, as Scripture says: "It depends not upon man's will or exertion, but upon God's mercy" (Rom. 9:16). Faith is a fruit of our union with Christ.

To know that we are united with Christ is to have assurance. True, the psychological awareness of personal assurance will vary from person to person, and for a given person from day to day. The strength of our faith is not always the same. But although the degree of assurance varies with the strength of one's faith, the security of salvation is a valid reality even for the person whose faith is weak. It is the gracious, sovereign, electing work of God which alone can account even for a weak faith.

To base salvation-security on anything other than God's completed work in Christ leads to uncertainty and distrust. If salvation-security depends on anything we do (for example, our faith), then we must constantly question the reliability of that action. And the reliability we need can never be found in our faith. It can be found only in the riches of the divine grace which never fails.

The personal act of faith is never flawless. It must not be

---

[4]*What is Faith?* (Grand Rapids: Eerdmans, 1946), p. 197.

presented as something on which our salvation depends. Our hope is in God. As paradoxical as it may seem, imperfect faith is evidence of our union with Jesus Christ. Even weak faith can assure of salvation. Warfield's eloquent comments on John 5:24 are worth quoting at length:

> What a blessed assurance, when faith is made thus not the ground of salvation, but its evidence! It is here that the sweet herb of election begins to pour forth its refreshing cordial. Men may tell us, indeed, "Believe and you will be saved," while still making faith the ground or the condition of salvation. And, then, with what dreadful solicitude will we pluck up our faith over and over again by the roots, to examine it with anxious fear. Is it the right faith? Is it strong enough faith? Do I believe aright? Do I believe enough? Shall I abide in my belief until the end? Dreadful uncertainty! Inexpressible misery and ineradicable doubt! It is only when we learn from such words of our Master as those before us today, that we dare to say to our souls not only, Believe and ye shall be saved! but those other words of deeper meaning and fuller comfort, caught from the Master's own lips: Believe and ye *are* saved! "Truly, truly, I say to you," says our Savior in words which sum up previous teachings, "he who hears my word and believes him who sent me, *has* eternal life; he does not come into judgment, but has passed from death to life."[5]

Calvin stresses that assurance of faith comes only by looking to Christ and trusting that we are accepted by God because we are members of the body of Christ. God loves us and gives us an eternal inheritance in Christ even as he chose us in him. "If we have been chosen in him, we shall not find assurance of our election in ourselves; and not even in God the Father, if we conceive him as severed from his Son. Christ, then, is the mirror wherein we must, and without self-deception may, contemplate our own election."[6]

Barth finds no pastoral emphasis in Calvin's view of election, which allows that there are some who are not elect. To posit the non-election of some, he says, is necessarily to foster anxiety. And so he looks for assurance of salvation in the fact that all persons are elect in Christ. A parallel claim is that, unless there is a

[5]*The Savior of the World*, p. 242.
[6]*Institutes*, III, xxiv, 5.

provisional salvation for everyone, there can be no assurance of salvation for anyone. "The real assurance for me that Christ died *for me* is this alone, that he died for absolutely *all,*" is the reasoning of the Lutheran theologian R. C. H. Lenski.[7]

"All persons are elect in Christ" would indeed be a solid basis for assurance of salvation, if such election involved actual salvation for all persons. This, however, Barth does not affirm. So again a solid basis for assurance exists if Christ's having died "for absolutely *all*" means that "absolutely all" participate in the salvation earned by Christ's death. This the proponents of *universalis gratia* do not acknowledge.

Does traditional Calvinism have any better basis for assurance? One formulation of the challenge which has traditionally been a thorn in the flesh for Calvinism is presented by Eric Gritch and Robert Jenson: If, as Calvinists say, salvation depends on the sovereign decision of God and God has not chosen to save all, then the gospel is true only for some people. From this they conclude, "Lutherans must ask: If I cannot be sure that it is meant for me when I hear it, how can it be *gospel?*"[8]

The response of biblical universalism is: "The gospel *is* meant for you unless you are indifferent toward it or wilfully reject it." Those who earnestly desire to know whether the gospel is meant for them must be told that any genuine longing or desire to be part of the kingdom of God is itself evidence of the renewing work of the Holy Spirit. Whatever else one may think of his theology, one must agree with Herman Hoeksema that apart from Christ there can be no turning to God.[9] Union with Christ is in no way accomplished by or contingent on the personal choice of the individual involved. Only in being joined to Christ does one become willing to receive redemption in his name.

It cannot be denied that the Calvinistic view of predestination has sometimes been presented in a way that leaves the impression that it is possible for someone to desire assurance of sal-

[7]R. C. H. Lenski, *First Epistle to the Corinthians* (Columbus, Ohio: Wartburg Press, 1937), p. 1029.
[8]Eric W. Gritch and Robert W. Jenson, *Lutheranism: The Theological Movement and Its Confessional Writings* (Philadelphia: Fortress, 1976), p. 161.
[9]Herman Hoeksema, *The Wonder of Grace* (Grand Rapids: Eerdmans, 1946), pp. 38f.

vation but not be able to achieve it because he or she is non-elect, or has no way of knowing whether he or she is elect. However, when it is understood that responsibility for non-election or rejection rests *entirely* with those who are non-elect, it is evident that it can never happen that a person who desires to partake of God's grace cannot do so. Those who refuse to come to Christ (John 5:40) have no one but themselves to blame. Jesus said that those who do come to him and those whom the Father has given to him are the same persons (John 6:37).

No one, however, may be so presumptuous as to think that he or she is in Christ — and thus assured of salvation — without having sorrow for sin and hungering and thirsting for righteousness. Those who say they are united to Christ will give evidence of that fact by the way they live. Berkouwer's reminder is to the point: "It is impossible to walk the way of certainty apart from sanctification. How would life, based on the electing grace of God, be possible apart from that sanctification which is the purpose of election?"[10]

How does one come to assurance of salvation? We must accept the testimony of God's Word. As we have been constituted sinners in Adam, so we have been made righteous in Christ:

> If you want to have assurance of salvation, the place to start is not with your feelings, but with your understanding; then the feelings will follow. The way to get assurance is not to try to feel something, but it is to grasp this objective truth. Look at yourself in Adam; though you had done nothing you were declared a sinner. Look at yourself in Christ; and see that, though you have done nothing, you are declared to be righteous. This is the parallel. We must get rid of all thought of our actions. There is no boasting. We do nothing; all we are and have results from the obedience of the one — our Lord.[11]

The apostle Paul had assurance of new life in Christ, "because one died for all" (see p. 43). Yes, all persons — except those who wilfully disregard the will of God — can rest assured that Christ has died for them and has thereby secured their salvation. This is the unconditional good news of the gospel.

[10]*Divine Election,* p. 301.
[11]D. Martyn Lloyd-Jones, *Romans: Exposition of Chapter 5, Assurance* (London: Banner of Truth, 1971), p. 274.

D. *Motives for Evangelism*

We do not intend to give an exhaustive list of the biblical motives for evangelism here, only to consider how the premise of biblical universalism is directly related to the incentive to carry out the Great Commission.

Because biblical universalism teaches that all persons are elect in Christ except those who reject the knowledge of God's will for them, it may seem at first glance to diminish the urgency for proclaiming the good news. In fact, some might even carry this to its logical conclusion and argue that, because all are elect in Christ except those who disavow God's will for them, it might be better if no one heard the gospel: the less they know of God's will, the less opportunity they have to reject it.

This line of reasoning overlooks the teaching of Scripture that every responsible adult is inclined by nature to suppress the truth that God declares to him through "the things that are made." Natural revelation is sufficient to convict people of sin and leave them without excuse (Rom. 1:20, 21), whether they hear the gospel or not. Furthermore, the Bible tells us that we are born in sin and captive to the law of sin (Rom. 7:23), inclined by nature to do those things contrary to the law of God "written on our hearts" (Rom. 2:15).

Biblical universalism takes seriously the real significance of the human ability to ignore the revelation God gives us (whether natural or special). There is a decisive power in human choice to refuse "to acknowledge God" (Rom. 1:28). Such refusal sets in motion a hardening process which culminates in condemnation.

As we examine the biblical data concerning this decision (the decision which must be made in response to God's revelation) we find that people have a choice to make. But it is not the power of contrary choice. By reason of the universal enslavement to sin, no one has the capacity within himself or herself to choose the good. No one can sovereignly decide to believe, since "no one can say 'Jesus is Lord' except by the Holy Spirit" (1 Cor. 12:13; see also Phil. 1:29; Eph. 2:8). Neither does Scripture know anything of a prevenient grace given to all persons to enable them to choose the good. The only decision of which a person is independently capable is the decision of unbelief: the disregard or rejection of divine revelation.

The church has been given the responsibility to do all it can to persuade people not to reject or remain indifferent to God's revealed will, to use the means given to it to persuade all persons to accept the testimony God has given of himself.

The only means revealed in Scripture which the Holy Spirit employs to work in the heart of mentally responsible adults, so that they will not close their eyes to God and turn away from their Creator and Redeemer, is the proclamation of the gospel. Whether God ever performs this same work by some means not revealed in Scripture must remain an unanswered question (see pp. 29f.). Paul says that "every one who calls upon the name of the Lord will be saved" (Rom. 10:13). Because we know of no other way of persuading others to repent of their sin, to believe, and to live in obedience, the appeal is properly addressed to our consciences by the question: "How are men to call upon him in whom they have not believed? And how are they to believe in him whom they have not heard? And how are they to hear without a preacher?" (Rom. 10:14).

Because we are aware of only this one means by which God works out his purpose of salvation in the lives of others, it is no wonder that we read, "How beautiful are the feet of those who preach good news!" (Rom. 10:15). Nothing is more apt to make people respond in repentance and faith to both the wrath and the goodness of God than the truth of the gospel. The cure for sin's self-destructive tendency is to look to "the Lamb of God, who takes away the sin of the world!" (John 1:29). Nowhere else can we see at the same time the ugliness of our sin and the astonishing light of God's redeeming love as clearly as in the cross of Jesus Christ. "For it is the God who said, 'Let light shine out of darkness,' who has shone in our hearts to give the light of the knowledge of the glory of God in the face of Christ" (2 Cor. 4:6). Understandably, therefore, Paul decided to know nothing among those to whom he was sent "except Jesus Christ and him crucified" (1 Cor. 2:2). The church must now preach this gospel to all persons everywhere, commanding them to repent, believe, and commit their lives to Christ.

The Bible reveals that a person in sin is only capable of

making a negative decision, the decision to disregard God and his will. In spite of this, it is not surprising that some traditions teach that the decision which people must make when confronted with the gospel is a free and sovereign decision to either believe or not believe. For all practical purposes, the child of God will experience the decision to believe as if it were his or her own sovereign free choice to believe. However, it is God who "is at work in you, both to will and to work for his good pleasure" (Phil. 2:13). Looking back on his experience every believer echoes this expression of gratitude:

> 'Tis not that I did choose Thee,
> For, Lord, that could not be;
> This heart would still refuse thee,
> Hadst Thou not chosen me.
> Thou from the sin that stained me
> Hast cleansed and set me free;
> Of old Thou hast ordained me,
> That I should live for Thee.

Biblical universalism has to do with motivation for doing the work of evangelism in another way. It is helpful at this point to note what Lester DeKoster says about the power of words:

> Yes, words are lenses, like those in our glasses. Love is a way of seeing — through the lenses set upon the eyes of the soul by God's words.
>
> An authentic and life-giving reading of the Bible equips the inner eye with the words through which we are to see. . . .
>
> What a lot of difference it makes, for example, whether we see another human being through the lenses of words like "enemy," and "alien," or like "neighbor," and "friend." Seeing is filtered through the choice of words we have laid upon the vital eyes of the soul. Are they God's words? Are they the devil's words? Or don't we know — or care?[12]

How do we view the masses of humanity — as strangers? or "outsiders?" Do we possibly think them to be enemies of the cross of Christ? Do you not know, or, perhaps, do we not care? Do we look on them as partakers with us of the grace of God in Christ Jesus?

[12]*How to Read the Bible*, p. 77.

Are we concerned for them, looking upon them as sheep who belong in God's fold? How does our picture of them relate to the work of evangelism?

Orthodox Christianity correctly holds to the view expressed by Verduin:

> The Bible nowhere teaches a universal redemptive fatherhood of God; it nowhere teaches a universal redemptive brotherhood of man. The redemptive fatherhood of God, according to the Christian Scriptures, extends as far as does the modality of savedness, and no farther. The human brotherhood of which the Bible speaks is a brotherhood that extends as far as the modality of savedness extends, and no farther.[13]

The practical application of this view forces us to make a determination as to how far the "modality of savedness" extends. Who are to be regarded and treated as brothers and sisters in Christ? All those who have been baptized, that is, all who are members of the covenant community of believers? All those who have publicly confessed their faith in Christ? To this question biblical universalism answers that God alone knows who are truly in "the modality of savedness." Therefore we must work on the basis of an assumption as to who are "elect in Christ" (see pp. 79ff.). The assumption with which we work is that all persons are elect in Christ *except those who the Bible declares will be lost.*

What a difference it makes to view others in connection with Jesus Christ! We should regard every person as a "brother for whom Christ died" (1 Cor. 8:11). This general approach of biblical universalism breaks down barriers between people. It promotes a feeling of interdependence and mutual concern. It helps overcome prejudices which arise out of fear because we view others apathetically or, worse still, with suspicion. We must look upon all persons with a desire to help them, even as our Lord taught us to show compassion for those who are straying, as the parables of Luke 15 demonstrate.

Biblical universalism puts lenses on our eyes so that we treat our fellow human beings as those for whom Christ died unless and until they by their indifference or continuing hostility separate themselves from us and from the Christ who lives in us.

[13]Verduin, *Somewhat Less Than God,* p. 79.

When we accept others as fellow heirs of the kingdom of heaven, we share with them the joy and the hope that is in Christ. We encourage them to live with us in joyful obedience to him as our Teacher, King, and High Priest. As we converse with those who have not heard the good news, we share with them that "in these last days" God "has spoken to us by a Son, whom he appointed the heir of all things, through whom also he created the world" (Heb. 1:2). We assert that we must pay close "attention to what we have heard, lest we drift away from it," for "how shall we escape if we neglect so great a salvation?" (Heb. 2:1, 3).

CHAPTER XIII

Unconditional Good News

> I do not believe in hawking either Christ or His merits. I do not believe in offering Him cheaply to anyone. But in moments of intimate converse with serious searchers I must have and I do have the freedom to set before them what Christ has done *for them*. Not: what He has done for them if they believe, but what He has done for them *as they are*. That is how I read Romans 5:8 and Romans 5:10. This affirmation is the heart and center of my ministry to men in the name of Christ. This is the gospel of Christ.[1]

THIS statement appears to be based on the premise that there is a message of unconditional good news which may be presented "to all persons promiscuously and without distinction, to whom God out of His good pleasure sends the gospel" (Canons of Dort, II, 5). Indeed, the framework of Calvinistic theology can be used to validate such a premise. On the one hand, if, as Calvinism teaches, there is an unconditional election to salvation, then surely unconditional good news is the essence of the gospel message. On the other hand, it cannot be denied that the gospel is to be proclaimed "to all persons promiscuously and without distinction."

The validity of this premise is jeopardized, however, when it is viewed from the perspective of the Calvinistic doctrine of particular atonement (Chapter VII). Christ did not provide salvation *for all persons* without any exceptions. Some Calvinists have thus maintained that unconditional good news may not be proclaimed to all persons promiscuously. Appealing to the words

---

[1]Harry Boer, "For Whom Did Christ Die?", *Reformed Journal*, XVI (May-June 1966), 19.

of the Canons of Dort — "The promise of the gospel is that whoso-ever believes in Christ crucified shall not perish . . ." (II, 5) — they say that there must be some evidence of faith before we can tell a particular individual that Christ died for him or her.

Others warn against the implication that the Canons of Dort teach a conditional salvation. They point out that the Canons do not say that *if* one believes . . . he shall not perish. Rather, the Canons make a statement of fact — the good news of the gospel is that "whosoever believes in Christ crucified shall not perish but have everlasting life" (II, 5). This statement is, of course, biblically indisputable.

To bring the good news to a particular person, however, we must apparently make a choice. Either we must wait for some indication of new spiritual life before declaring what Christ has done for that person, or we must proceed in our evangelistic ap-proach on the basis of some form of *universalis gratia* (the teaching that Christ provided salvation for all persons, including those who will not be saved).

The years 1962 to 1967 witnessed an extended discussion in the Christian Reformed Church concerning this dilemma. The discussion centered on the question of whether it is theologically permissible in communicating the gospel to use the expression "Christ died for you." Many thought such a statement would be inappropriate without some prior evidence of Christ's redemptive work in the person addressed. Others were willing, if need be, to accept the existence of some form of divine redemptive love for all persons. Because this lengthy — and eventually unresolved — dis-cussion brought to the surface many of the critical issues we have been considering in this book, and because biblical universalism would seem to provide the key to solving the real theological prob-lems which do arise in communicating the good news to those who have not heard, we shall devote some attention in this final chap-ter to this piece of history. We shall keep the practical aspects of the debate in sharp focus, hoping thereby to lay to rest the charge that Calvinism has no "theology of approach" applicable to the realities of Christian witnessing.

Interestingly, the majority of those who were most di-rectly involved in evangelistic outreach intuitively felt that it was necessary and proper to make a positive declaration of God's redeeming love in approaching individuals with the message of the gospel. They could not, however, convince the church that there is biblical warrant for such a declaration in evangelistic outreach. In response to the proposed recommendation that the use of the phrase "Christ died for you" be discouraged, one conference of missionaries unanimously adopted the following statement:

> As missionaries we feel that . . . it is one of the beauties of the Gospel and one of the joys of preaching to be able to preach to individual sinners and assure them that Christ gave Himself as a sacrifice for the sins of particular individuals. . . . Proscription of this phrase ["Christ died for you"] would truncate our evangelistic preaching. We need to say this in our preaching so that men as individuals feel individually drawn to the Loving Savior and make an individual commitment of repentance and faith.[2]

The first objection raised by the denominational committee appointed to study the matter of presenting unconditional good news to all persons was that "only through acceptance of Christ by a true faith, and thus also through a consequent union with Christ, will anyone be a partaker of all the love and grace that are found in Him."[3] The committee concluded that because true faith is necessary before anyone can become a partaker of the fulness of Christ's benefits, we may therefore never say to anyone "Christ died for you" until that person has given evidence of having true faith.

Although this objection was stated as self-evident, it is neither precise nor factually true. Its imprecision gives it plausibility. It is factually in error because there are elect children who die in infancy and do "partake of all the love and grace that are found" in Christ without ever having exercised or expressed true faith as that term is used here. This is important, because the objection implies that true faith *establishes* union ("a consequent union") with Christ.

We must state once again that whenever Scripture sets forth the necessity, the urgency, the *sine qua non* of saving faith, the context is always that of normally responsible adults to whom the gospel is proclaimed. As we saw in Chapter IX, this urgency

---

[2]*Acts of Synod* of the Christian Reformed Church, 1967, p. 493.
[3]*Ibid.*, p. 578.

does not arise because faith establishes or leads to the vital union between Christ and the elect. This union is rather the fruit of the gracious, sovereign, divine act of election to salvation from before the foundation of the world. The necessity and urgency of faith stem from the fact that all mentally responsible persons who do not believe the message of the gospel thereby reject it. It is this human act of rejection that brings about damnation.

The imprecision of this first objection is found in the word "partaker." True, capable adults to whom the gospel comes can know and experience the joy, hope, peace, and blessedness of their justification only by way of a self-conscious act of faith. "No sinner accosted by God in Christ through the *kerygma* can really know whether Christ died for him except in the constancy of believing commitment to the spoken word of God."[4] But do we conclude from this that we must refrain from telling the sinner that Christ died for him or her until we see some evidence of belief that this is so? If Scripture does not (and therefore we may not) declare that Christ died for him or her, on what evidence or testimony is the belief that Christ died for him or her to be based? Such a circular approach hinders an effective witness.

The committee's second objection was that "it is not proper to say to all men without distinction, 'Christ died for you.' For such a statement is not verifiable, and may be untrue of many who hear the gospel."[5] There is a certain biblical warrant to this observation: Jesus taught us not to "give dogs what is holy; and do not throw your pearls before swine" (Matt. 7:6). For messengers of the gospel to shake off the dust from their feet against those who will not receive them or listen to their words is not an idle threat (Matt. 10:14; Mark 6:11; Luke 9:5; 10:11; Acts 13:51). But just because some prove themselves *unworthy* of hearing the good news, we may not for that reason withhold the word of peace until there is a demonstrated *worthiness* to receive it.

The only reason some need for not using the expression "Christ died for you" in their evangelism endeavors is that it "may be untrue of many who hear." This appears to be a formidable argument at first sight. But its weakness is evident in this response:

---

[4]A. C. DeJong, *The Well-Meant Gospel Offer*, p. 174.
[5]*Acts of Synod*, 1967, p. 581.

If I cannot say to every man that Christ died for him because some of those to whom I speak may be lost, then I can also not say to every believer that Christ died for him because some of them may in the end prove not to be elect. The history of the Church is replete with men and women who after having given every reason to be counted as believers died in unbelief and infidelity. [If] . . . the words "Christ died for you" can be addressed only to the elect, since only God has final knowledge of who the elect are, we can therefore say "Christ died for you" to no man.[6]

In the early church, as in the church today, there were unregenerate members. Some of them received baptism, partook of the Lord's Supper, and at times held some of the most important offices in the church. There were false brethren, false teachers, and even false apostles (see 2 Cor. 11:4ff.; Gal. 2:4; John 6:66; 1 John 2:18ff.; 1 Tim. 6:20, 21). In no way was it verified that all the members of the churches established by Paul were elect persons. Nevertheless, Paul did not hesitate to identify himself with the members of the visible church, declaring to them that it was Jesus Christ "who gave himself for *our* sins" (Gal. 1:4).

If a person's actual election must be verified before he or she can be addressed as being "in Christ," the warrant for addressing a Christian congregation as "Beloved in the Lord Jesus Christ" is the likelihood that at least some within that assembled body are elect. But then how can the sacrament of baptism be administered to any particular individual, either infant or adult? Who is the searcher of hearts who can determine that the grace of God which is signified and sealed in baptism is a verified reality in the recipient? If verifiability is the needed criterion, how can a presiding pastor invite "each of you" to partake, repeating our Lord's words: "This cup is the new covenant in my blood, even that which is poured out for you" (Luke 22:20)? "This is my body which is broken for you" were the words addressed by Jesus to Judas among others (see Belgic Confession, Art. XXXV). How can verifiability be possible in any instance in which it is said "Christ died for you"?

Some would reply that verifiability is not required in the instances cited. To persons partaking of the sacraments we are

[6]Boer, *loc. cit.*, p. 18.

warranted in declaring "Christ died for you" because they profess to be the recipients of God's grace. If God's grace is not a reality in their lives the responsibility for the mistaken declaration lies with them. But this reply hardly meets the objection as we cited it above, which is if it "may be untrue," it is not proper to say "Christ died for you." It "may be untrue" of any professing Christian. We must conclude that, if the objection is valid, we can *never* use the expression "Christ died for you."

A third objection voiced by the committee was that the statement "Christ died for you" is not found in the preaching of Christ or the apostles. To this the following reply is to the point:

> This is hardly an argument against the validity of making such a statement to unbelievers. For, as a matter of fact, such a statement is not even used in the Bible as an address to believers. Yet does anyone question that it may be properly so used? The Bible gives us general principles which must be applied to the life and work of the Church.[7]

If the premise of Scripture is that all persons are elect in Christ except those who Bible declares will be lost, then the church ought to formulate this truth in such a way that it can be meaningfully presented to individuals as well as to groups of persons. The unfortunate result of the objections we have discussed so far is a certain hesitancy in proclaiming the good news. The Dutch theologian B. Holwerda has rightly lamented:

> We no longer know what preaching is. For one person it is a deep discussion, for another it is a devotional exercise. But it is actually an announcement of acquittal. It is the witness of the forgiveness of sin, not just an explanation of the work of Christ, or even a discussion of how we can share in that forgiveness. It is rather a proclamation that we share in that forgiveness. Here you are not told that you can receive forgiveness of sin, nor how you can receive that forgiveness, but it is said that your sins are forgiven you. John writes to the congregation, "My little children — your sins are forgiven you for his name's sake!" That is preaching, declaring the judgment of God.[8]

This hesitancy and lack of forthright proclamation "de-

---

[7]*Acts of Synod*, 1967, p. 581.

[8]B. Holwerda, *De dingen die ons van God geschonken zijn* (N.V. Goes, Netherlands: Oosterbaan and LeCointre, 1954), pp. 160f.; my translation.

claring the judgment of God" has a dulling effect on the Word preached. The problem is evident in preaching which takes place within the church, by electronic media, and in print. The reluctance to include all who hear within the scope of the universalistic texts is evident not only in preaching but also in witness to individuals. Many sincere orthodox Christians believe they may not say "Christ died for you" in the sense of a universal provision for the salvation of all persons, even for those who will not ultimately be saved. Yet since these people do sense the need for such a declaration, they make it hesitantly—with a qualification attached.

Consider Bavinck's report of a conversation between a nonbelieving Chinese language teacher and a missionary, as they concluded the reading of Luke 23. The Chinese instructor asked: " 'Why had Jesus to suffer all this?' The missionary replied: 'He gave His life for you and for me.' The Chinese teacher asked: 'For me also?' The missionary said: 'Yes, also for you, if you believe in Him.' "[9]

One wonders why the missionary's answer to the second question was not simply "Yes," since he had already told the teacher that Christ had given his life for him. Surely the extended answer was true. But any number of extended answers would have been *equally* true: "Yes, also for you, if you keep Jesus' word" (John 8:51); "Yes, also for you, if you deny yourself, take up your cross, and follow him" (Matt. 16:24); "Yes, also for you, if you serve Jesus" (John 12:26); "Yes, also for you, if you consider yourself dead to sin and alive to God" (Rom. 6:11); "Yes, also for you, if you will present your body a living sacrifice, holy and acceptable to God" (Rom. 12:1); "Yes, also for you, if you work out your own salvation with fear and trembling" (Phil. 2:12); "Yes, also for you, if you walk not after the flesh but after the Spirit" (Rom. 8:4); and so on.

All the above extended responses convey the biblically expected, required, demanded *outgrowths* or fruits of God's saving grace working in our hearts. None of them, including *faith*, is a condition, basis, or activating device which enables us to receive God's grace. All the above responses are involved with each other. Faith cannot be exercised or exist apart from the various responses

[9]J. H. Bavinck, *The Impact of Christianity*, p. 163.

of works: "What does it profit, my brethren, if a man says he has faith but has not works? Can his faith save him?" (James 2:14). "You see that a man is justified by works and not by faith alone" (James 2:24).

It is true that all who hear the gospel must believe. Without faith it is impossible for them to be saved. All those who desire to receive the righteousness of Christ and make it their own can do so in no other way than by faith alone (only), according to the Heidelberg Catechism (Q. 61). It should be remembered, however, that the catechism is drawing the distinction between a righteousness acquired by doing works of the law and that which comes in the way of faith so that it rests on grace (Rom. 4:16; cf. p. 90).

The faith by which one is justified is never *alone*. "So faith by itself, if it has no works, is dead" (James 2:17). Faith alone, that is, faith by itself, is dead. Whenever one adds the phrase "if you believe" to "Christ died for you," the impression is given that faith is the one condition which must be met in order to be a worthy recipient of God's mercy. Faith is then regarded as that one work or act of which all persons are capable — they need only be persuaded to exercise their ability to believe. The conditional proclamation of the good news in such phrases as "Christ died for you, if you believe" and "if you believe, you will be saved" is based on the presupposition that all persons are outside of Christ except those who the Bible declares will be saved. Such conditional proclamation implies that some *essential* human act or attitude is required to establish us in the state of grace.

Certainly there is a legitimate and useful purpose for the expression "if you believe" when presenting the gospel, but only when one means thereby to convey the need for a life of obedience as a child of God. It is improperly used if it conveys the idea that faith is the one prerequisite demanded of the sinner so that God may save him or her. For all practical purposes there is no difference between calling someone to obedience and calling that person to faith, since the exercise of faith is itself an act of obedience. "For I will not venture to speak anything except what Christ has wrought through me to win obedience from the Gentiles, by word and deed" (Rom. 15:18; see also Rom. 1:5).

Such a life of obedience, the obedience of faith included,

is not the condition for but the fruit of salvation. The call to live in total obedience to the will of God is addressed to members of the covenant community because they are "in" the covenant (Chapter X). The same call with the *identical requirement* comes to those who are "strangers" to the covenant, in order that they may become members of that covenant-keeping community. The call to a covenant-life response of repentance, faith, and joyful obedience comes to all who hear the gospel; and this call finds its validity and appeal only on the assumption that those so addressed are "in Christ."

Those who heard the message in New Testament times recognized that the call to faith was a summons to an entirely new kind of life, just as foreign missionaries today report that for a convert to receive baptism makes that person "a marked man." When Paul and Silas told the Philippian jailer to "believe in the Lord Jesus" (Acts 16:31), this was a call to live in fellowship with God, just as Abraham was called to "walk" before the face of the Lord (Gen. 17:1) — the very word "walk" implies total life commitment — because the Lord had covenanted with him and given him good news. Both the call of Abraham and of the Philippian jailer were unconditional. A total response was required of both men. Abraham's "believing" was the response required of a member of the covenant community, and the jailer's "believing" brought him into fellowship with that community.

It was "the blessing of Abraham" that came to the jailer (Gal. 3:14). The blessing Abraham received extended to his descendants after him (Gen. 17:7); similarly, the covenant promise and the sign of that promise are given to the jailer and those of his household (Acts 16:31-33).

This call to covenant life is unconditional good news. Succinctly stated it is: "Christ has died for you; therefore you must live as a child of God." The biblical terminology is: "One man's act of obedience leads to acquittal and life for all men" (Rom. 5:18). This unconditional good news is for all persons, and therefore the call goes forth to all to "consider [themselves] dead to sin and alive to God in Christ Jesus" (Rom. 6:11). The good news the church must bring to all people is this: He died for all; therefore you must live for him! (cf. 2 Cor. 5:15).

But one may object that to say to an unbeliever "God

loves you" or "Christ died for you" without adding the qualification "if you believe" will make that person complacent and give him or her no reason or incentive to change his or her way of living. Hundreds of years after the Reformation the doctrine of unconditional sovereign grace is still subjected to the charge that it may make people indifferent and wicked (Heidelberg Catechism, Q. 64). But who can say that, upon coming to know and understand the amazing truth of God's forgiving grace, freely and unconditionally given solely on the basis of Christ's merits, he or she became indifferent to God's will for life? Why then hesitate to proclaim that good news unconditionally to others?

Again it is objected that statements such as "God loves you" and "Christ died for you" are valid only for those who are "in Christ," that is, for the elect. So they are. And since there is no way to distinguish between the elect and non-elect in bringing the good news, one can effectively, meaningfully, and forcefully proclaim the gospel to everyone only by assuming that all persons are elect in Christ except those who the Bible declares will be lost.

Finally, we must face the real cause for hesitancy about bringing the unconditional good news of redemption in Christ to all persons. What about the non-elect person to whom we say "God loves you" or "Christ died for you?" This much can be said: The very proclamation of this good news will one day testify against that person. Beyond that, we see only "the mystery of lawlessness." There are questions here which no one can answer and about which the Scripture is silent. This is that area of inquiry relating to "no man's land" (Chapter VII). The mystery of sin and unbelief poses questions most safely and solemnly left in the hands of God.

Having considered the objections raised against the use of the words "Christ died for you" in our evangelistic outreach, we should now ask what is the advantage of using the unconditional approach.

First of all, if one does not feel free to say "Christ died for you," one finds oneself in the awkward situation of inviting, asking, and even demanding of others that they believe something one does not feel free to declare to them. When the Scriptures say, "Believe in the Lord Jesus, and you will be saved," this is a call to the one true faith in which all believers are joined together. An ingredient of that faith is a trust or confidence that "not only others, but I too, have had my sins forgiven, have been made forever right with God, and have been granted salvation," in the words of the Heidelberg Catechism (Q. 21). This is precisely what all those who hear are asked to believe when the gospel is presented to them. How can one be asked to believe that one's sins are forgiven if there is no scriptural warrant for telling that person that Christ died for him or her? It is not enough to know that Christ died for sinners. One must believe that "not only others, but I too, have had my sins forgiven" and "have been made forever right with God."

"Preaching," says James Daane, "unlike mere talking, debating, lecturing, or theologizing, presents the truth of the gospel as truth and good news *for every hearer,* as something to be believed, accepted — the preacher must even persuade him to do so — on pain of being damned if he does not."[10] Holwerda also speaks to this issue:

> I believe the forgiveness of sins, because God promises me that. God acquits me before I believe. And Paul is correct that God justifies the ungodly. My faith is never first; the promise is first. Otherwise my faith becomes a shadow in the air, and my faith has nothing to grasp. The promise of forgiveness — that is, God's acquittal — goes before faith. . . . If I had to begin with faith, what could my faith hang on to? But his word of acquittal is there first.[11]

Another reason for assuming that all those to whom the gospel is presented are elect in Christ is that the Bible teaches human inability to respond to the truth except by the miracle of grace. Berkouwer observes regarding 1 Corinthians 12:3 ("No one can say 'Jesus is Lord' except by the Holy Spirit"): "The message of Scripture repeatedly accentuates that human inability. The impotence of man is not something pessimism has discovered; it is most literally described in Scripture (see John 3:27; 1 Cor. 2:4; Rom. 8:5-8)."[12]

The scriptural teaching that Christ is the vine and that apart from him we have no spiritual life implies that we must be

---

[10]James Daane, "Another Look at Common Grace," *Reformed Journal,* XV (Feb. 1965), 20.

[11]Holwerda, *op. cit.,* pp. 161f.

[12]*Divine Election,* p. 49.

united with him.[13] "This union is absolutely first. Unless the living connection is established between Christ and our inmost heart, we are outside of Him, and outside of Christ there is only guilt and damnation. . . ." In these words Herman Hoeksema correctly observes that the effects of our union with Adam must be overcome by a union with Christ. Those who are saved have died with Christ. He goes on to say that before there can be any new life in us that union must be accomplished:

> It is an absolute prerequisite for the reception of all salvation. For Christ is our all, and all our salvation is in Him. But we cannot begin to draw our life and light, our knowledge and wisdom, our righteousness and sanctification from Him, until our inmost heart is joined in spiritual unity with Him, who is the revelation of the God of our salvation.
>
> But how is this union accomplished? The answer of Scripture is unequivocal: this union is unconditionally and absolutely the work of God's grace in Christ Jesus. By grace are ye saved! That implies, too, that by grace, and by grace only, you are incorporated into Christ, so that you become one plant with Him.[14]

Those who genuinely and earnestly seek to persuade others of the truth of the gospel, and who pray that they may elicit a response of obedience and faith from their hearers, must do so on the assumption that those who are the objects of their concern are elect in Christ. Apart from such a union with Christ there can be no spiritual harvest.

It is true that Ezekiel was commanded to prophesy to dead bones which were "very dry" (Ezek. 37:2). The point of the vision, however, is that Ezekiel was commanded to regard those bones and to deal with them as if they were living and as though they could well hear and could and would respond. He was not to assume that they were dead; nor was he to assume that he could not be sure whether in fact they were dead or alive. He was commanded to take a positive approach toward them. He was told to prophesy and make demands of them as though they had the ability to discern what he was talking about. He was commanded:

---

[13]For a thorough exposition of the phrase "apart from me you can do nothing" (John 15:5), see Luther's *The Bondage of the Will*, pp. 259-66.
[14]Hoeksema, *The Wonder of Grace*, pp. 38f.

"Prophesy to these bones, and say to them, O dry bones, hear the word of the Lord" (vs. 4).

There is an additional reason for proclaiming the good news unconditionally. It is all but impossible to preach the gospel to a group without at least creating the impression with the hearers that Christ died for them. And, of course, whatever may be told a group may also be said to an individual in it. As James Daane says,

> I have read many accounts of how the gospel should be preached without saying, or appearing to say, to each hearer that God loves him and Christ died for him. We have been told that the gospel must be preached to all as a group, yet its content is only for the elect; or, in a way that differs only in words, that it must be preached to all men as a generality, while its special message is only for particular elect men. Yet these explanations are always slippery and evasive; none of them is satisfactory, unless one is satisfied with mere verbalism. We may be thankful that Jesus taught that the gospel can be preached not only to "all nations," but also to "every creature." This means that whatever the act of preaching is, it can be done to the single individual as well as to a group. This consideration rules out an elusive, slippery definition of preaching which plays out its definitions between the dialectics of the "one and the many." The gospel announces its message and calls men to decision, and the message that is the object of decision is the same for all.[15]

What Christ had done, and therefore what Paul preached to the church at Corinth, was of "first importance." Paul did not learn what Christ had done by observing *the response* of the Corinthians to the message he brought. Paul says explicitly that he *received* this good news as a truth of Scripture. This was something which Paul knew, therefore, and was commissioned to declare to the Corinthians *before* he had ever set foot in the city of Corinth. This is the truth that Paul "delivered" to them, namely, that Christ died for their sins as well as for Paul's own sins. "For I delivered to you as of first importance what I also received, that Christ died for our sins in accordance with the scriptures" (1 Cor. 15:3).

What an exciting, amazing, joyous, dynamic message

[15]"What Doctrine of Limited Atonement?", *Reformed Journal*, XIV (Dec. 1964), 16.

Paul was privileged to bring to the members of the church at Corinth! But where in Scripture did Paul find authorization to declare the good news to those living in Corinth that Christ had died for their sins? Paul was taught by Christ to understand the good news of salvation, the gospel he was to preach (Gal. 1:11, 12). He had been given a message that had relevance not for the Corinthians only, but for all persons, as he indeed states time and again in the universalistic texts of his letters, one of which is in this very chapter: "For as in Adam all die, so also in Christ shall all be made alive" (vs. 22). Here is the gospel which is to be preached everywhere. Here is the unconditional good news which permits us to identify with everyone who will hear us and say: "Christ died for our sins" according to the Scriptures.

No wonder the heavens were radiant with the glory of God the night Jesus was born, for this was the joyous unconditional proclamation heralded by the angel, the "good news of a great joy which will come to all the people [not "to the whole people"]; for to you is born this day in the city of David a Savior, who is Christ the Lord" (Luke 2:10, 11). One may object that the expression "the people" here is a special reference to the Jews as the people of God. So be it. This observation takes nothing away from the joyous distributive universalism of the unconditional good news. For Simeon, with the Holy Spirit upon him, while looking at the baby Jesus can say that his eyes have seen God's salvation, which has been prepared "in the presence of all peoples." This is a light for revelation to the Gentiles, as well as the glory of God's people Israel (Luke 2:30-32). This is the unconditional good news the church is called upon to proclaim to all people: to you there was born that day "in the city of David a Savior, who is Christ the Lord." Therefore, "yield yourselves to God as [those] who have been brought from death to life" (Rom. 6:13).

Subject Index

Textual Index

166